STOICISM

A Modern In-Depth Beginner's Guide on Stoic Principles to Help Transform Your Life by Fortifying Your Mindset, Gaining Confidence Through Emotional Resiliency, and Mastering the Art of Happiness

Walter Wayne

© **Copyright** 2021 - All rights reserved.

The content contained within this book may not be reproduced, duplicated or transmitted without direct written permission from the author or the publisher.

Under no circumstances will any blame or legal responsibility be held against the publisher, or author, for any damages, reparation, or monetary loss due to the information contained within this book, either directly or indirectly.

Legal Notice:

This book is copyright protected. It is only for personal use. You cannot amend, distribute, sell, use, quote or paraphrase any part, or the content within this book, without the consent of the author or publisher.

Disclaimer Notice:

Please note the information contained within this document is for educational and entertainment purposes only. All effort has been executed to present accurate, up to date, reliable, complete information. No warranties of any kind are declared or implied. Readers acknowledge that the author is not engaged in the rendering of legal, financial, medical or professional advice. The content within this book has been derived from various sources. Please consult a licensed professional before attempting any techniques outlined in this book.

By reading this document, the reader agrees that under no circumstances is the author responsible for any losses, direct or indirect, that are incurred as a result of the use of the information contained within this document, including, but not limited to, errors, omissions, or inaccuracies.

TABLE OF CONTENTS

Introduction 1

Chapter 1: Foundation 6

Chapter 2: How to Develop a Mental Toolkit from Stoic Philosophy 28

Chapter 3: Applying it to Daily Life 48

Chapter 4: Criticisms to Stoicisms and Counterarguments Against Those Critiques 69

Chapter 5: Preparing Practices 82

Chapter 6: Situational Practices and How to Handle Yourself When Challenged by Other People 100

Chapter 7: Stoicism in Pain Management 116

Conclusion 130

References 134

Image Sources 138

INTRODUCTION

Raven

Hardships and pain enter your life as quickly as they leave, and what you are left with is the task of piecing together what happened to you. Knowing how to be okay amongst that hardship and pain is a skill and an artform—this is Stoicism. As you learn how to process the difficulties that come your way, you can develop an inner strength that will allow you to heal faster and move on to more positive stages of your life. Stoicism is not the denial of these difficult moments that happen to you; it is the ability to handle them with grace and ease, which is a task that is not always simple.

However, you can learn how to be more Stoic in your everyday life. Through the concepts provided in this book, you will understand how to apply these principles to any difficulties you face.

Stoicism is not a brand-new concept. It has been around since the very early ages of history, forming a foundational approach to handling life that humans still use resourcefully today. Not to be confused with a hardened approach, Stoicism has many redeeming qualities that will make you more in touch with your emotions. Many confuse being Stoic with not caring or having denial about a situation, but it is quite the opposite—Stoicism teaches you how to fully understand your emotions and how to handle them.

Everything you go through, whether it is good, bad, or neutral, affects your mental health and well-being. There are many upsetting things that can happen to you, and the way you react is either going to make you or break you. To have good mental health, you need resources to help get you through certain situations and circumstances that try to break you. With the help of the useful steps in this book, you will discover how to create your own mental "toolkit." This is a collection of actionable steps you can take when you feel that your mental health is declining; it is a plan of action meant to serve you and uplift you. With this mental toolkit, you will no longer feel that certain parts of your life are way beyond your control. Instead, you will be able to figure out how to navigate your feelings and act in a way that is in your best interest.

However, Stoic principles do not only apply when you are in difficult situations—they turn into good habits that you can use all the time. When you learn how much they will benefit you, they will feel just as natural as any other form of self-care you practice. From handling communication with your spouse to working with people you find abrasive at your job, maintaining a Stoic mindset is going to help you manage your personal and professional relationships and your own emotions. It will give you a chance to focus on what is most important in your life because you will no longer be worrying if you are doing the right thing or acting the right way. With Stoicism, these guidelines of behavior and habits are laid out in a clear, concise manner that is easy to follow and understand.

Because so many aspects of life can be confusing and unclear, Stoicism feels like a breath of fresh air. It is a direct and outlined lifestyle choice that you can make. If you are ready to stop overreacting when your emotions get the best of you and letting discouragement ruin your self-confidence, then you are ready to begin implementing these principles into your life. All that is required of you is the desire to change and effort to make it happen—the rest comes with practice and consistency.

Imagine that you are making a commitment to your life right now, that you want to bring forth more joy, happiness, and positivity.

There are many other essential reasons why learning how to be a Stoic is important. When you apply the principles of

Stoicism into your life, you will experience these benefits:

- a rise in your confidence levels
- the ability to be emotionally resilient
- an understanding of how to achieve happiness
- a clear and concise mindset that guides you
- being an inspiration to others
- caring less about the opinions of others
- wasting less time on what is unimportant
- relief from the anxiety you experience regularly
- an expanded feeling of gratitude for what you have

If you are thinking this concept sounds too good to be true, you will be given the chance to think rationally about Stoicism and understand how it can truly help you achieve the above benefits.

In this book, you will discover the criticisms and counterarguments about this lifestyle choice so that you will be able to make the best decision for your life. Without hearing both sides of any story, you are not giving yourself a fair chance to think rationally. This is what sets this book apart from the rest. Filled with valuable Stoic principles, you are also given the chance to take a transparent look at what it means to be a Stoic individual and understand any drawbacks.

Before you apply any major change to your life, you must believe that it is going to benefit you in some way. As you read on, think about these principles and how you could realistically apply them to your life and routines. See if you can picture yourself as a Stoic individual, unscathed by the hindrances that once debilitated you in the past. The time to rise above is right now, and if you are ready to do so, this book is going to teach you exactly what must be done.

CHAPTER 1

FOUNDATION

Ancient

Stoicism is synonymous with strength. It empowers you to become a strong person with grace, endurance, and humility. Instead of waking up in the morning and groaning about all that must be done, you will learn how to feel thankful for what you get to experience. Stoicism shifts your perspective and teaches you how to become a more mindful individual. This, then, affects your life in many ways, from the way you act professionally to the way you carry yourself personally. It is an all-encompassing lifestyle choice that you can embrace.

Key Beliefs and Core Philosophies

Prayer

The main belief in Stoicism is that you must always keep a calm and rational mindset, no matter what is happening in your life or what you are going through. This serves the purpose of giving you a better understanding into outside events and your internal thoughts and emotions so that you can focus on only what you can control instead of what you cannot. This, in turn, allows you to feel more peaceful. Stoicism can help you let go of the worries that you tend to hold onto from the things that happen to you.

What follows are some of the core philosophies of Stoicism. These should be the guiding principles in the mind of someone who wishes to live a Stoic lifestyle. Through adopting these principles into your own life, you will discover how to achieve their benefits.

- **Live in Agreement with Nature** - To become one with Stoicism, you must become one with nature. In Stoicism, Eudaimonia is roughly translated as the ultimate happiness that can be attained. What Stoicism implies is that human beings are rational animals. Being a human involves knowing the difference between right and wrong and making the distinction between the two through our core values. We also have reason and higher knowledge—those who are Stoic believe this is what separates us from animals.

    Remember, we are unique and different from every other species of animal. When we get in touch with the more natural elements of life, it is thought that we are better able to function as human beings.

- **Live by Virtue** - The highest good in Stoicism is known as virtue. It is thought that when you believe you are living according to virtue, you are living the Good Life. Those who are Stoic classify their virtues into four categories known as the four cardinal virtues, which are: Wisdom or Prudence (good judgment, understanding perspective, and good sensibility), Justice or Fairness (kind-hearted behavior, benevolence, dealing with situations fairly, and acts of public service), Courage or Fortitude (bravery, authenticity, and confidence), and Self-Discipline or Temperance (self-control, forgiveness, and humility).

Using all these virtues as guides, you can make progress on your path toward the Good Life. According to Stoic principles, you can only achieve virtue when you live by all the above cardinal virtues. When you get through your days with humility, when you use good judgment, and when you act with a kind heart, you will know that you are on the right track.

- **Focus on What You Can Control and Accept What You Can't** - To abide by a Stoic lifestyle, you must be able to determine what is up to you and what is not. When something is within your power, it is worth your energy and focus. Mainly, your actions and judgments are what you should be paying attention to because those are normally voluntary. Some examples of what is not up to you include death, health, reputation, outside events, and other people's actions.

  To see this clearly, you must be able to define the difference between the things that are voluntary and involuntary. Ideally, the thought of letting go of what you cannot control should bring you peace. Because you know that this stressor cannot be changed, you can focus your energy on positive things.

- **Take Action** - The Stoic lifestyle is not one that includes being passive. It is thought that you must always take action when you can. This is the "warrior mentality." Laziness does not apply to those who believe in Stoic principles because they only see laziness as an excuse—there is always time to do something if you deem it important enough. You always have options, but you might have to brainstorm to get there. These are only some examples of ways that people who are Stoic think.

You are encouraged to take action because this will help you make progress on your journey. If you can do something that will get you closer to your end goal, why wouldn't you go ahead and take action? While it sounds easier than it is, you must rely on your determination and willpower to turn this into a daily reality.

- **Practice Misfortune** - Stoic people think about the idea of what might go wrong. They do not do so in a disruptive manner but to prepare for anything that might happen. The point is, you never know what is going to happen, even when you can control all your known factors. Whenever you make a choice, your end result may turn out exactly as planned, may turn out horribly, or may end up with a neutral outcome.

In Stoicism, premeditation of adversity is essential. Think of it like softening the blow if the outcome is not a good one. Those who are Stoic always aim to handle situations with grace and effervescence; this helps them to do so. Instead of seeing misfortunes as a negative, it is better to see them as things you are indifferent about. This will take a lot of mental capability and practice.

- **Add a Reserve Clause to Your Planned Actions** - What this means is that you are aiming to live the Good Life and abiding by the highest virtues, but you must still accept all outcomes with calmness and composure. Someone who is Stoic does not believe in losing their temper when things do not go according to plan. Instead, they will turn it into a lesson that makes them stronger.

As long as you have done your very best to succeed and understand the factors that you have control over and those you don't, the rest is going to happen as intended. You must deal with this rationally. An example of a reserve clause is this: "I will get into law school, as long as nothing prevents me." This is an awareness of a goal ("I will get into law school") but also a simultaneous acceptance of outside factors you cannot control ("as long as nothing prevents me").

- **Love Everything That Happens** - Events will happen in your life that you find unfavorable and unpleasant. These events are in the past, though. You cannot do anything to change the experience you had. Sure, you can make improvements to prevent the same thing from happening again in the future, but you should never dwell on what has already passed.

In Stoicism, there is a notion called the "art of acquiescence." This means to practice acceptance instead of resisting every little thing. This is going to help you find peace with and within the situations that happen to you. While you might not *love* getting into an argument with your partner, you can learn to accept that it happened and move forward with your life. This is also going to help you find solutions for the problems you wish to fix.

- **Turn Obstacles into Opportunities** - This one is fairly self-explanatory, but it holds the same weight as the rest of the Stoic principles: The way you perceive situations is how you are going to react to them. When you reach an obstacle in your life, you did not decide that this should happen, but you do get to decide how you will proceed. You can either let the obstacle overpower and hinder you, or you can turn it into a learning opportunity.

Those who are Stoic perform the latter. They see obstacles as opportunities every chance they get. To do this, you must get into the right mindset. If you are in a negative one, you won't be able to see your obstacles as anything other than personal attacks to your ego. Not everyone or everything is out to get you.

- **Be Mindful** - To someone who follows Stoic principles, they realize that not everything revolves around them. Though certain situations involve them, they might not be the main focus. Being mindful of your surroundings and your place in them will enlighten you. It can make you realize that certain things aren't as big of a deal as you think they are or don't truly affect you, and, in turn, you will be met with some peace of mind.

If you already consider yourself a mindful individual, great! What being Stoic will do for you is enhance this quality. To be mindful, you must monitor your actions and behaviors closely. Examine why you come to the conclusions that you make and what leads you to your final choices. You will learn a lot about yourself through mindfulness. In each instance that you act, try to focus on exactly what your intentions are.

The Three Stoic Disciplines

Since the beginning of Stoicism, its principles have emphasized three main topics: ethics, physics, and logic. These and the three stoic disciplines discussed below are the guidelines for maintaining your path to Stoicism and are based on the lessons of Epictetus, a Stoic teacher whose work is among some of the only to survive from those ancient times. There are four volumes of his *Discourses* that were recorded from lectures. There is also his famous Stoic handbook, known as *Enchiridion*, that you can read to learn more about the three Stoic disciplines.

- **The Discipline of Desire** - This discipline has to do with accepting your fate. It applies to your daily life and almost any situation in it, even ones that do not cause you conflict. Your fate is what is meant to happen to you—it is a part of something that has already been planned out by a higher power. According to the Stoic view of living in harmony with nature, it is thought that you must have a philosophical way of thinking to accept the discipline of desire.

- You must learn to realize that your fate is necessary; it is inevitable. Much like worrying about the things you cannot control, trying to change your fate will not do you any good in life. It is only going to cause you upset and will waste your precious time and energy. Instead of trying to seek out specific events to happen in your life, you should turn your focus on wishing positivity for the events that are fated to happen to you. By *accepting* that these events are occurring or will occur, you can hope for the best and put good intentions behind each one by using your positive mindset and outlook.

Do not confuse this acceptance with weakness. Stoics are not weak by any means. They do not simply accept wrongdoing with open arms. There are always limits and exceptions to any discipline, so you must use your knowledge and rationality to determine when you must stand up for yourself or try and alter your circumstances. If something is happening to you that is harmful or very terrible, it makes sense that it is going to be a lot harder to accept your fate. This is when the Stoic need for action kicks in—you will want to take actionable steps to improve your life.

Stoicism is very much about choosing your battles, and some are not worth fighting. If you are going to waste your positive energy, then the choice becomes apparent—you should not fight this battle. Knowing how to use your self-control to prevent yourself from engaging in wasted fights can be difficult. So many people have a fight-or-flight response that tells them to fight instantly. Not everything has to be so confrontational, though. Imagine how much better your life will feel when you are void of all conflict.

Those who are Stoic combine two unique traits: the ability to accept what is happening and the courage needed to take action. These two traits create a great balance in how one can live life to the fullest.

- **The Discipline of Action** - When you feel the need to take action, you get an impulse that tells you something must be done. However, it might not always be apparent what action should be taken, even though the feeling remains. This impulse can drive you to make a good decision or it can cause you to make a bad one. Through the Stoic discipline of action, you need to figure out which impulses to act on and which to leave alone.

Stoic ethics prepares people for knowing what is inherently good and what is bad. As an individual, you have an idea of this yourself. When you are faced with a situation where you feel the need to act, think about your knowledge about good and bad. These things align with your personal beliefs, and they should be very meaningful to you. The more you follow your intuition on what is considered good or bad, the closer you are to living the Good Life.

Don't forget that certain events in your life can also cause indifference. If you feel indifferent to something, this does not need to be a situation you overthink. It is okay to remain neutral and to let the situation be. Just as it is encouraged to let yourself be, knowing when to refrain from taking action is an advanced Stoic discipline that you will learn. It does involve a sense of self-control, but it also encourages you to activate your intuition.

When it comes to other people and taking action, it is a Stoic belief that you must always wish others well. If you were to act on a vengeful impulse toward another person, this would be considered very bad. The thoughts that you have for your fellow humans should be nothing but kind and positive, no matter who they are or what they have done for you. What you have to understand is that not everyone is receptive to the action you want to take. If you do something for someone and they do not appreciate it, they might be unaware of the effort you are putting into the action. You cannot let this get the best of you. Do kind things for others because you truly want to take positive action, not because you want to be rewarded.

When you act, you need to feel good about it, even if it was difficult to get through. This can be a hard principle to learn, but it will help you in the long run. Feeling proud of and comfortable with your actions is going to make your life better. It will allow you to emotionally process life events and your own feelings better, which clears up valuable space in your mind, as you are not worrying about the past.

- **The Discipline of Assent** - When you must make judgments, this discipline trains you to do so with meaningfulness. A judgment that must be made with intention, like deciding whether to go out to dinner or stay in and cook, is something you can apply this discipline to. You might rationalize that you deserve the luxury of going to a restaurant, but you can also argue that staying in and cooking would save money and be more practical. You must live within your own essential harmony by doing what is best for you without harming yourself or others. The concept makes a lot of sense, and it involves being mindful of every decision you must make.

This discipline falls in line with the trait of wisdom (the better your judgments, the more wisdom you gain). Stoicism principles contain the belief that you have the ability to make the best choices for yourself. If you do not know what should be done, look inward for some insight. Through what you know about yourself, you should be able to choose the right action or make the right choice. With the continual awareness of your true self, if you are ever faced with the same or similar situations in the future, you can use the experiences and the knowledge you already have to help you decide what must be done. This discipline also requires that you must take accountability for your actions, refraining from blaming outside factors if things do not turn out as planned.

Of course, you are going to encounter some irrational judgments from time to time, but your mindfulness will make you aware of them. For example, you should not judge someone else's appearance because you find it unfavorable in your opinion.

Additionally, you should have control over the vices that tempt you. If you quit smoking and are craving a cigarette, your better judgment will kick in to tell you that the feeling will pass and that you should not smoke. This Stoic willpower is what makes its believers such strong people. Even if the desire is very hard to overcome, this should be your goal. Work through the temptations to lead yourself to a place of contentment.

By continually evaluating your judgments, even if you have made them countless times before, Stoicism suggests that you will be able to spot any unhealthy behaviors before they manifest into bad habits. If this were to happen to you, it is said that you must withhold your "assent" rather than being carried away by the poor judgments.

The Four Passions

In Stoicism, there are four main passions, which are lust, fear, delight, and distress. These passions are what can prevent you from achieving a Stoic lifestyle. In Stoicism philosophy, you must avoid these passions, as they can lead you astray and cause you misery.

Lust

The Stoics define lust as a disorder of desire where you focus solely on the goodness or pleasures in your future. Lust, basically, makes you want to possess all the good thoughts, feelings, or events of your future all at once. However, striving for all these lustful things can backfire on you. It's important to understand that lust does not only pertain to your romantic life, but it comes in many different varieties that show up in all aspects of your life.

Varieties of Lust	**Definition**
Anger	This is lust as a form of punishment. You might punish a person who you believe hurt you undeservingly.

Rage	This is a type of anger that can show up sporadically. It can make you feel very intense feelings because it is unexpected.
Hate	Hatred is a habit that is formed. It is a constant disdain for something that makes you feel negative.
Enmity	This is another type of anger. It is an active anger that is waiting for an opportunity for revenge.
Wrath	An intense type of anger, wrath contains a lot of bitterness that you hold onto internally. You feel it inside of your heart and soul.
Greed	This is a lust that feels insatiable. You might desire money or belongings in abundance.
Longing	This lust is a yearning feeling that applies to someone or something that is not present.

Fear

This disorder arises from having an expectation of something evil or inherently bad happening to you or others. You might feel threatened and unstable because of this fear. It can cause you to act differently because you might become standoffish or retreat from people or situations.

Varieties of Fear	Definition
Sluggishness	You might become sluggish when you are afraid of a difficult or arduous task you must complete. As you tread carefully towards it, you might even sense doom.
Shame	This is a fear of others thinking that you are a disgrace. It is rooted in disappointment.
Fright	This is a paralyzing fear that can cause paleness, physical trembling, stomach upset, and stress.
Timidity	Because you are worried about evil approaching, you might act timid as a way of being careful. This provides you with a sense of false security.

Consternation	We all have a mental balance, and this is a fear of upsetting that balance. When something doesn't feel right in your mind, it can manifest in your actions.
Pusillanimity	This is a lingering feeling that often follows fright. If you are already frightened, this fear makes you worry that something else negative will occur.
Confusion	When you are fearful, your thoughts can be paralyzed or frozen. This can make you feel uncertain about yourself and your surroundings.
Faintheartedness	This is a long-lasting fear that might present as a dull feeling always in the back of your mind.

Delight

A positive passion, delight occurs when you feel pleasure in some way. This happens when you are in the presence of an apparent good, whether that is a person you care about or a material possession that makes you feel happy. When you feel delight, you normally feel secure and content, as well. However, too much delight or the wrong variety of delight can be disadvantageous, as delight can come from a negative place, emotion, or situation.

Varieties of Delight	Definition
Malice	This is when you feel delight that is derived from something evil. It does not bring you any advantages.
Rapture	This occurs from a delight that you hear, which soothes your soul. In a way, you are entranced and charmed by it, but it may not help you think clearly.
Ostentation	This is an outward expression of delight that causes you to act extravagantly. You might even become boastful and overconfident, which aren't positive traits.

Distress

This stems from a newly formed belief that there is evil present. It is the kind of feeling that can shrink you, causing you to feel vulnerable and unsure about what will happen to you. It might also affect you mentally and physically, leading to depressive behavior.

Varieties of Distress	**Definition**
Envy	When another person has something that you desire, you might feel a sense of longing. This might do you harm, however, depending on how you react to it.
Rivalry	If someone has something, whether a person or thing, that you want as well, this creates tension. In your mind, that person may become your enemy.
Jealousy	This is the feeling of distress that takes over when you realize someone else has something you desperately want.
Compassion	This feeling can translate to pity. You are overcome with distress while watching someone else who is going through undeserved suffering.
Anxiety	This is a type of distress that feels oppressive. It can often become debilitating, causing you to question your actions and thoughts.

Mourning	When you encounter the untimely death of a loved one, you enter a period of mourning. This kind of distress can linger with you for a long time, often coming up when you least expect it.
Sadness	A familiar feeling for most, sadness makes you feel down both physically and mentally. It can also make you feel like crying.
Trouble	This is when a burden occurs. You often feel that you do not know how to handle this type of distress because it creates a disruption from what is normal for you.
Grief	This is a slow, torturous type of distress. You can grieve a loved one's death or even the figurative loss of a friend for a long time.
Lamenting	When you experience this, there comes a period of waiting. It is a sadness that lingers, but you must wait for it to pass on its own.

Depression	A powerful force, depression can stop you in your tracks, affecting you emotionally, mentally, and physically. It also comes with an element of brooding.
Vexation	A constant distress that doesn't seem to go away for a long period of time. When you feel this way, it can feel like it is not temporary.
Pining	This is the distress that comes with the element of physical bodily discomfort.
Despondency	When you feel this, you are distressed with no resolution in sight. You might lose hope because it does not seem like there will ever be a solution, so you settle into the feeling.

History

History

Stoicism began in ancient Greece. It was originally a Hellenistic philosophy that was founded in Athens around 300 B.C.E. and was influenced by Socrates and Cynics. Vigorously, its believers debated with the Skeptics, Academics, and Epicureans. The philosophy was brought to Rome where it began to flourish during the period of the Roman Empire. It was not always seen in a positive light, though. Some Emperors disliked it, while others lived by its principles.

Stoicism's influence, however, was undeniable. This unique philosophy was even powerful enough to shape Christianity. You can see this influence through the fact that, just like Christianity, Stoicism sits on the foundation of the practice of virtue, and it is only through virtue that you can achieve true happiness.

Scholars recognize three main branches of Stoicism. First,

there is Stoa, which was founded by Zeno of Citium. He originally founded this school of thought in 300 B.C.E.

Second, there is middle Stoa, notably practiced by Panaetius and Posidonius in the late II and I century B.C.E.

The final branch is from the Roman Imperial period, known as late Stoa. Seneca, Musonius Rufus, Epictetcus, and Marcus Aurelius practiced this form of Stoicism during this time period.

If you recognize any of those names, you are likely familiar with the very ancient beginnings of Stoicism. It continues to fascinate scholars today because it has been so well practiced throughout the ages. Although the principles have become more modernized in recent times, its underpinnings are still the same. You can become a Stoic, too, if you decide to apply them to your life.

CHAPTER 2

HOW TO DEVELOP A MENTAL TOOLKIT FROM STOIC PHILOSOPHY

Thinking

Your mental health is arguably as important as your physical health. A mental toolkit is a resource you can use to maintain optimal mental health. Even if you are not struggling in life, it is still a good idea to create one in case life gets challenging, as it often does. Plus, just having your mental toolkit makes you feel more secure.

Stoicism is the perfect foundation for creating a mental toolkit. Brimming with helpful principles, it allows you to make a plan for maintaining a sound mind. In turn, this will help you in every other aspect of your life. The tools in your mental toolkit are the exercises and practices that guide you toward making the best decisions possible. When incorporating Stoicism into the toolkit, you will be on the right path toward the Good Life.

Thinking Like a Stoic

Calmness

When you have a setback in life, you essentially have two options: suffer from it or experience it. While you might not have an enjoyable time changing your flat tire, it is still an experience you can gain value from. Instead of complaining about how life always gets you down, you can change your tire and get to where you were going.

This is how you rise above adversity; this is how you think like a Stoic.

To change your perspective, you must practice the art of reframing your way of thinking. This occurs by looking at a situation you already made a negative judgment on and seeing its positive qualities instead.

In Stoicism, Seneca was encouraging to his followers—he urged them to try to look at the positive side of all situations, no matter how terrible they first appeared. In ancient Stoicism, they believed that the gods were in control of all human affairs. Any loss or distress you experienced happened because you caught the deities' attention. They also believed this was Jupiter's (who was the king of the gods) way of putting your character to the test. In a way, encountering a setback can be considered an honor because a higher power believes you are strong enough to overcome and learn from it.

Even if you do not believe in gods, deities, or any higher power, you can find something within that is bigger than yourself. Think about how you are not in control of every single aspect of your life. Often your life is left to chance, luck, and maybe fate. The parts that you cannot control happen for some reason, according to the Stoics. Next time you are faced with a challenging situation, stop and think about the way that you are well-equipped to get through it. With all the tools and knowledge you need, you will navigate the path back toward the Good Life.

Some setbacks will only be minor, others major. When you hit your shin on the coffee table, this is an example of a minor setback. It is temporary, and it doesn't disrupt your entire day. While it hurts a lot momentarily, you are able to get through the pain and continue with what you were doing. This is the exact way you can aim to view the larger setbacks in your life, like getting fired from a job or going through a breakup. While these instances hurt a lot more mentally, you can still find the power within yourself to make your way through them.

You can also have the major setback of experiencing negative emotions, but they do not have to overtake you. It isn't wrong to feel angry or upset when something bad happens to you; this is normal and natural. Allow yourself to feel these things, but do not lose focus of your main goal: getting through the moment. Because that is what a setback is, only a moment of your life. In a year from now, it will be a distant memory. The longer you allow yourself to stew in your negative emotions, the harder it becomes to break free from their binds. Imagine they are passing through, only stopping to check-in with you as a reminder of why you need the motivation to continue onward.

As mentioned, humans are both rational and animalistic. There is a strong need to survive, but it can be accompanied by difficult mental symptoms that can feel nearly impossible to overcome. You are in control of your mind, both the animal and rational parts, and you can use it to the best of your ability. With Stoic thinking, you can turn your problems and negative emotions into lessons that make you even better and even stronger. Even if you become upset momentarily, something is always going to shift. There will be a breaking point where rationality steps forward and allows you to see that better days are ahead for you.

The rational part of your mind is the most dominant. You can likely deduce that you will survive a terrible situation, even if emotions are trying to tell you otherwise. When the environment of your mind is controlled, rationality reigns. Take away this control, and the animalistic component comes out. If you experience anger, fear, or hatred, it is tempting to forget about your principles and to act out those feelings by projecting them. Whether you mistreat yourself or other people, this is an unhealthy action for you. It is only going to make the negativity seem worse.

According to the Stoics, setbacks can trigger the animalistic instincts we all have inside. This does not mean we must act on them, though. With some self-control and regrouping of our thoughts, it is possible to closely follow the principles that were detailed above. Getting your rational thinking pattern back, you will feel stronger and more capable of overcoming what you are going through. The negativity will still feel present, but it will not be able to take you down with it.

To practice the Stoic way of thinking, try the following exercise:

1. Realize that you are experiencing a setback. Whether you feel angry, afraid, upset, or any other negative emotion, know that your animalistic impulses are kicking in.

2. Imagine that there are "Stoic gods" who are responsible for the setback you are experiencing. This is deliberate and controlled, a test for you.

3. Instead of letting your impulses take over, bring

some rationality back into your thinking. Understand that the gods know you can handle this situation or else they would have never presented you with it.

When you use this strategy, any problem becomes a little smaller. You will feel more capable of handling it with grace and humility. Instead of giving into your emotions, you can better manage your life by tapping into your mental toughness. This is what your mental toolkit will be used to enhance. Any time you feel that you are in danger of giving into an impulse, remind yourself of how strong and resilient you are. Think about what a Stoic individual would do in the situation.

Given time, you might find that you actually look forward to setbacks in some ways. These challenges are meant to test you, and you know that you will have the necessary confidence to see yourself to the other side of them. It takes practice to get to this point in your life, but it is entirely possible for you to achieve this mindset. Allow yourself to explore the boundaries of what you once thought you could not handle. These challenges do not control you; the one in control is the one with a strong mind.

Unlike other philosophical beliefs, Stoicism is more than a moral philosophy. It is a set of psychological tools, perfect for your mental toolkit.

Stoic Beliefs on Various Topics

Cemetery

The Stoics have their own unique beliefs about ordinary events and topics that we all encounter in our lives. Their mindset, however, is based on the principle of finding the benefits in every situation. Their beliefs can help you process and understand regular life occurrences.

Death

In most Stoic texts, death is a recurring theme. This is because death is a natural part of human life. Many people you know will die in your lifetime, and it is important to be able to process this loss. The ones who die will be people you love, people you need.

The saying "memento mori" translates to a symbolic reminder that death is inevitable. Instead of using this saying in a fearful way, however, the Stoics transformed it into a tool to guide themselves and others through the process of handling death. They do not wish to forget that their time on Earth is limited.

To conquer the fear of death, the Stoics use it productively and see it objectively—it is recognized as a natural fate that we all meet. Seneca wrote, "We have entered the kingdom of Fortune, whose rule is harsh and unconquerable, and at her whim, we will endure suffering, deserved and undeserved." This was Seneca's response after losing his son. He acknowledged that people we love will die, and it will hurt us. This is not meant to hinder us, however.

Most assume that Stoics are notorious for suppressing their emotions, but they simply process them in a different way. Their philosophy teaches us to face, process, and deal with the outcome immediately. When you hold onto any type of negativity, such as grief, it will hinder you in the days of your life to come.

Desire

The four Stoic passions are divided into two categories: things that are not in present possession and things that are anticipated. The idea of desire falls into the latter category. Epictetus stated, "Freedom isn't secured by filling up your heart's desire but by removing your desire." It is a statement that reflects on how longing for too much can keep you from living a productive life. To experience true freedom, you must maintain your desires in a healthy way in order to successfully manifest them.

Instead of waiting, hoping, and wishing for something great to happen to you, taking actionable steps will lead to results. Human beings tend to desire a lot but change their behavioral patterns very sparingly. You cannot expect to meet new people by remaining in the same social circles. Stoicism urges us to broaden our horizons; this is the only way to implement true change.

Wealth

Modesty is another tenet of Stoicism and is the lens in which wealth is viewed. For example, Seneca was a wealthy Roman aristocrat, but he still chose to live a modest lifestyle. Just because you have it all does not mean you need it all—this can be a tough lesson to process when greed is so prominent among the human race. There is nothing in Stoicism that inherently states that wealth must be avoided. If you have it and want to indulge in it, you can do so while remaining humble and full of integrity. Your actions as a result of your wealth are what matter most.

Irvine states, "Stoicism does not require one to renounce wealth; it allows one to enjoy it and use it to the benefit of oneself and those around." As long as you are not greedy or boastful, you have every right to be grateful for the wealth that you earn. It is suggested that you not only use wealth for your own benefit but for the benefit of the people in your life, as well. This is how you can remain humble.

Pleasure

Although some believe that the Stoics reject all pleasure, this is not true. They do not outwardly reject all pleasure, only pleasure that is reckless or dangerous. As you know, not all the things that make you feel good are good for you. Stoicism warns to be careful of this, while also remaining aware that it is okay to revel in joy. They encourage you to become your own source of satisfaction. If you spend time waiting for pleasurable moments to take place, you might grow frustrated or upset when the results you are looking for do not come to fruition.

Epictetus quotes Socrates in saying, "Just as one person delights in improving his farm, and another his horse, so I delight in attending to my own improvement day by day." It is no surprise that the Stoic lifestyle encourages you to find your happiness within. When you rely on other sources too much, this is when your pleasure can manifest into something negative, such as greed or jealousy. Find reasons to feel pleasures that do not involve material items or outside factors first.

What Others Think

"Tranquility comes when you stop caring what they say. Or think, or do. Only what you do." —Marcus Aurelius

So much of your time is likely spent worrying about what other people think of you. Are they going to like your outfit? Will they see you as a great candidate for this job? However, these thoughts about what others think can become very troublesome if you let them take over your mind. This can also create a great deal of anxiety, stopping you from making any progress. You might even lose sleep over the hypothetical "what-ifs" you consider while lying in bed at night.

How other people feel is outside of your control—remember that. You also cannot choose their actions. What you can control is what you choose to do. This means you can either let their words or actions hinder you, or you can rise above these opinions and do what you know is right. With the Stoic principles guiding you, making the right decision shouldn't be difficult. Only stress over what you know you can control. This is how you grow as a person.

Emotion

While Stoicism appears to be a philosophy void of emotion, it is the exact opposite. The truth is that Stoic individuals just process their emotions quickly. They still feel all the emotions that other people do and welcome them with open arms, even the difficult ones; it's just that they do not hold onto them for long periods of time. They can identify them and discern what they mean. This leaves room for them to take action quickly.

The goal is to regulate your emotions, not to prevent yourself from feeling any. First, by understanding what is causing your distress, you will be better able to get started with processing your emotions. Any unresolved feelings will prevent you from progressing in life.

Do not dwell on your emotions. Experience them for what they are worth, then decide what to do with them. It is a straightforward approach to taking on some of life's toughest challenges. When many would crumble under pressure of many emotions, a Stoic remains calm and graceful to handle them in the way they know best.

Mental Toughness

In Stoicism, there is a sense of "toughing it out" when you

experience something negative. Being tough in situations that challenge you will better allow you to handle them. It isn't always easy to adopt this mindset, but it does make you stronger in the end. Make sure your focus is on always bettering yourself. If you consider that being strong in a hard situation will make future negative situations easier, then this can motivate you to stay strong in the present. Train your brain to do this at all times, even when you do not feel like it.

One of the best times to train is when you are already uncomfortable. This allows you to push past the need to let yourself off easy and slip into lazy habits. Embrace the fact that life is testing you. As described, Stoics believed that life challenges were gifts from the higher powers above. Somehow, it is known that you can survive whatever it is that you are going through right now. Be proud of yourself for how far you have come and how much you have left to accomplish—you can do this.

Stoics believe in each person having unique abilities or powers. Find yours and use them to your advantage. If you have any special skills or traits that help you with your mental toughness, do not hesitate to incorporate them into your routine.

Material Possessions

To a Stoic, material possessions are not a priority. However, they do not need to be banished or denied. Stoicism is much more than what you have; it is what you know and how you carry yourself. Stoics value pragmatism and are always thinking about ways to help others and better themselves. If you happen to be wealthy in possessions, it is important to use them wisely. If a material item is no longer of any use to you, then you can donate it to someone in need or can simply get rid of it, if it has no value to others.

Having clutter in your home will provide you with distractions. Simply being able to see the clutter is something for your brain to focus on rather than focusing on yourself or your issues. You will see disarray, and that can cause disarray in the mind. A lingering, disordered thought that bothers you will not subside unless you suppress it or take practical action. The same is true with possessions: Disordered or too many possessions require action. And in Stoicism, you always want to take action.

Happiness

Stoics believe that happiness comes from within. Even if something outside of yourself is causing you happiness, you are able to feel it because of the personal work you have done within yourself. The happier the person, the more enlightened they are. This means they know who they are and what they believe in. Understanding what you stand for in this world is very important. You will become an unhappy person if you do not have any standards or morals. Those who are always miserable likely have no concept of who they are as people. They see negativity and take it as a part of themselves when they do not need to. Keep your beliefs close to your heart, always remembering to stand up for what you believe in and to point out any injustices.

In Stoicism, while happiness can be obtained through outside sources, the most valuable happiness is the kind you create for yourself. This happiness comes from doing something good for another person or setting a goal for yourself and completing it.

Virtue

As you know, virtue is one of the most important qualities to possess if you want to practice Stoicism. When you live by virtue, you are doing the very best you can, and you are on the path to the Good Life. This standard of moral excellence can be applied to any aspect of your life. Make sure that you have virtue on your mind as you make your way through each day. Without its guiding force, you might end up feeling lost or unsure of what to do next. Virtue is like a compass that will show you the way.

To live a virtuous life, you must always maintain good judgment by using your wisdom. There are temptations on every path in life, but you control whether or not you give into them. The more you practice living a virtuous lifestyle, the wiser you become. In turn, you can pass on your wisdom for the greater good of helping other people. This creates a domino effect of positivity in your life. Always aim for the choices that will lead you to the greater good—they will not fail you.

Adversity

Everyone is going to face adversity in life. The challenges you go through can either destroy you or make you stronger. To a Stoic, adversity is a tool that can be used to enhance your life skills. It is an honor to be challenged in this way, and it is not something to fret over or to feel fearful about.

When faced with adversity, consider what you already know about yourself. Think about what you can do right now about the situation to alleviate some of the burdens. Once you start brainstorming, other ideas will follow.

A lot of people give into adversity because they feel stuck or powerless. In Stoicism, you will never put yourself in this position of defeat. Because you have free will and wisdom, there are always going to be options available to you. Even if it takes work to search for them, it becomes worth it in the end when you are able to rise above the very thing that was trying to bring you down. Adversity cannot be more powerful or stronger than you are, not when you have the knowledge of the Stoic principles in your mind.

Mental Illness

With mental illness comes debilitating symptoms. If you are mentally ill and attempting to follow the principles of Stoicism, you may have some difficulties but that doesn't mean you should give up on the practice. Some mental illnesses, such as anxiety disorders and depression, simply do not allow you to "get over" things in the way that Stoic beliefs suggest you can. This is a hindrance that you must face, but it will not be impossible to bring the Stoic belief system into your life.

The best things in life take a lot of hard work, and this will be one of them, if you so choose.

Because Stoicism has such a focus on following through and with productivity, it is compatible with mental illness in a positive way. Though it might not be as simple for someone who is suffering from mental illness to practice these principles, the Stoics believed that they can apply to anyone. While their ancient views might be insensitive in today's modern world, they saw mental illness as yet another burden to face and to overcome. In some ways, that is exactly what a mental illness is: something that can be faced and treated. Everybody needs to take as much time as they need to truly heal, though, and you should get professional help, if needed.

Acting Like a Stoic

Smart

The following examples illustrate how you can incorporate the practice of Stoicism into your life right now. While it takes time to discover what works for you, these examples will guide you toward the right path. If the modern world is becoming a lot for you to handle, switching over to these Stoic practices can help you make sense of everything.

1. **Guard Your Time** - The time you have is precious and valuable. Do not give it away to just anyone. If you know that something isn't worth your time or

attention, you do not have to agree to do it. Stand up for yourself by recognizing that you can choose the actions you take.

2. **Don't Outsource Your Happiness** - If you merely wait around for other things or people to make you happy, this puts you in a fragile state of being. You need to find your own ways to make yourself happy. Discover who you are and what you like. Have confidence in yourself and in your abilities.

3. **Stay Focused When Faced with Distractions** - In the modern world, distractions are constantly around us, but it is important to stay focused. When you give in and interact with something distracting, this takes you further away from your goal. Remember why you are completing the task in the first place.

4. **Rid Yourself of Ego and Vanity** - These are two traits you do not need in your life. For one, they drain you of energy that you can spend on better behaviors and thoughts. These traits could make you unlikable or superficial as well. Acting in an egotistical and vain manner can make it difficult to get along with others, too.

5. **Put Your Thoughts in Writing** - Thinking constantly about what you have done during the day, what is still left to do tomorrow, and what you have to do in the weeks or months to come can make you feel scattered and stressed. Even thoughts about relationships and work issues can clutter your mind. When you feel jumbled up inside, write down what you are thinking. Journaling is a wonderful practice

that can be used daily to clear your mind and center yourself. It will also serve as a reminder of your goals, desires, dreams, and responsibilities.

These five tasks are simple enough to incorporate into your life, yet they still guide you in a very positive direction. Turning something into a habit takes at least 21 days, so give them some time before you decide if they are suitable for you. Don't give up on your goal of a Stoic lifestyle easily—make a commitment to bettering yourself and give yourself the time to do so.

Examples

Concepts

Reading about the principles and practices of Stoicism is only one part of studying the philosophy and learning how to apply it to your life. The next part is understanding how it can help real people in real-life situations. The following examples will show you how Stoicism works in today's world.

Stoicism and the Pandemic

This is a trying time for many people all around the world. As a collective, humans are experiencing a pandemic that few could ever imagine possible. With all the unknowns surrounding this event, it is natural to feel a heightened sense of uneasiness and insecurity. But Stoicism can help you get through the uncomfortable and distressed feelings that the pandemic has brought out in you.

It all comes down to knowing what is in your control and what is outside for your control. Of course, this pandemic is outside of your control. It happened quickly, and it still continues to change the course of your daily life. Never knowing what is going to happen next or when it will get better, you must take on an approach that allows you to understand that you alone cannot fix this. It is the Stoic principle of handling your reaction to the stressor that helps during this time.

Because Stoicism trains you to deal with anything that happens to you, it is the perfect philosophy to utilize in trying times like these. There is still so much uncertainty in the world, but practicing Stoicism can bring a little security back into your life by providing you a solid foundation. While the world might not feel "normal" right now, you can still manage your internal feelings and make the best decisions for yourself and others.

Stoicism and Reduction of Anxiety

A graduate student in India, Anika, felt the need to tap into some ancient practices to deal with her anxiety and procrastination issues. These negative behaviors had so overtaken her life that she was not able to get anything done, and this then made her feel even worse about herself. Anika was given two rituals based on Stoicism that were designed to help her face these problems:

1. Take an ice bath or cold shower three times each week.
2. Negative visualization for 10 minutes each day.

She was to do these two rituals for a six-week period.

The ice baths were meant to help her observe how her mind reacted before, during, and after a surprising or unexpectedly unpleasant event. Because this induced her anxiety on her own terms, she was able to learn how to control it.

Procrastination is related to anxiety in the way that it can feel outside of your control. When you view procrastination from this perspective of control, however, you can then convince yourself to jump into your task (like an ice bath) before you spend too much time debating the benefits of doing or not doing what you know you must. After all, you are in total control, not your feelings of procrastination.

Negative visualization is imagining the worst possible outcomes that could happen to you in your life. When you think about the reality of the situation, though, and compare it to your negative visualizations, you see that your life is a lot happier and a lot better than you might have originally thought. This practice teaches you how to appreciate what you have and to express gratitude; it could always be a lot worse.

CHAPTER 3

APPLYING IT TO DAILY LIFE

Morning

Having confidence in life is incredibly important, and the Stoics were best known for their straightforward and confident demeanors. They carried themselves this way because of the deep internal understanding they had of themselves.

Taking an ancient philosophy and applying it to your daily life is not as daunting as it may seem. These principles are still so relevant in today's society that integrating them into your routine is not only possible but rather simple. Through doing so, you will feel a shift in consciousness. Newly aware of all your actions, this mindfulness will translate into benefits in your personal life and professional interactions.

Cultivating Positivity

Knowing that the mind is much more than a receptive device, you can mold it to adopt more positive habits and strengthen the quality of your behaviors. Below, are some methods for cultivating positivity:

- **Keep a Thought Journal** - Each time you encounter a negative thought, write it down without placing any judgments on yourself for why you are feeling this way. You can jot down simple words and statements about the way you feel. Give yourself reminders of what caused the feeling.

  For example, maybe your coworkers all go out for dinner after work ends, and you are the only one who does not get an invitation. This will surely cause you to feel discontent in some form—jot it down. After a full week of writing, review all your negative thoughts and feelings in order to understand your current mindset.

- **Test Your Core Beliefs** - Using your thought journal, identify one situation that caused you negative emotions. With the above example involving your coworkers, you can dissect the situation. Think about the very worst thing that can happen. Be as specific as possible. You might concur that your coworkers all dislike you because they view you as a bad person. While that is likely untrue, your mind might tell you that this is why you did not get an invitation that night.

Next, you need to make a contract with yourself to put this theory to the test. When you get another opportunity to socialize with your coworkers, test how they respond to you. This will show you what they actually think.

When your coworkers ask you how your weekend went or what you like to do in your spare time, these are both pros that you can add to your list of reasons why they probably do not dislike you. You might find out that they only thought you were busy that night or there was a mix-up with the invitation where everyone thought that you were already invited.

- **Label Your Thoughts** - After you have completed the first two steps, your awareness of your negativity will be at an all-time high—this is the beginning stage of mindfulness. Instead of gravitating toward judgment, once again, you must take a non-judgmental approach to reduce the power of your negativity.

You can tell yourself that you had a thought your coworkers hate you. Choose to accept this as merely a thought that crossed your mind, not a solid belief or truth. Your history and past beliefs shape your thought patterns. These beliefs are not always true because they are based on subjective instances you have experienced.

- **Thought Stopping** - Thinking negatively can cause very quick downward spirals that make you feel you are out of control. Once you let your mind run away with a negative thought, it is only going to get lost in it. This exercise is meant to reclaim even more of the power of your own thoughts.

  As soon as you notice yourself falling back into a negative thought pattern, simply tell yourself "stop." Say it out loud if you can. This might seem trivial or comical, but it will claim your stance on the way you feel about negativity entering your life. Your strong feelings of wanting this cycle to stop will interrupt the thought pattern, which is exactly what you need to do. Make it your goal to turn this into a new habit.

- **Change Your All-or-Nothing Beliefs** - No matter how you think, you should not be thinking in terms of absolutes. Situations are not only going to contain an option one and an option two. There is a big space in between that is filled with numerous possibilities. Eliminate the words "must," "none," "never," "always," "ever," and "nobody" from your vocabulary.

  For example, instead of saying, "None of my coworkers like me," you can say "I have an opportunity to get to know my coworkers to see if we are compatible as friends."

- **Develop a Positivity Bias** - Even while doing your

best to stop your brain from focusing on negative thought patterns, there is more you can do—it is now time to develop a positivity bias. Essentially, this is the habit of looking at the bright side of all situations you encounter.

Confirmation bias is a well-known psychological phenomenon where people only take in and accept ideas that are already aligned with what they believe and will dismiss ideas that are contrary to their beliefs. Confirmation bias, however, can be used to help people banish their negative-leaning thinking.

If you are convinced that your coworkers do not like you, then you will find every reason you can to confirm this. However, if you make yourself believe your coworkers do like you, then you will find more reasons and examples that back that up. By switching to a positive viewpoint, you can bring more positivity into your life, while also understanding that your negativity is only rooted in fear, insecurity, or past experiences.

Practicing Emotional Resilience

Emotions

Emotional resilience is a skill that the Stoics are best known for. Through practice, you can also become more emotionally resilient in your life. The main thing to remember before attempting to work on your skills is that there is a difference between emotional resilience and avoidance or denial. If something bad happens to you, practicing emotional resilience does not mean ignoring this fact or suppressing the feelings you have about it—you still need to process your emotions, even if they happen to be negative. Life isn't only going to present you with perfect moments and positive encounters; there will be times when everything seems like it is working against you.

True emotional resilience is your ability to adapt to stressful or distressing situations. As mentioned, what matters more is how you react to stress and less how you internalize it. Even in crisis, you can teach yourself how to be calm and collected, coming up with valid ways to get through the moment. In the end, that is all it is—a moment that is temporary. Your biggest problems in life are not going to follow you for the entirety of your existence; although, it can sometimes feel this way. When you encounter a major problem today, it might end up being insignificant by the end of the week.

Depending on what you are going through, it can take you some time to truly feel emotionally resilient regarding the situation. This is okay because there is no deadline to impose on yourself. You must give yourself time to properly handle and identify what you are feeling; this is the only way you are going to find solutions that work for you. Also, everybody is different. Emotional processing is such a unique experience because of individual personality traits, childhood upbringings, and past emotional instances.

You are probably familiar with the saying that you must "roll with the punches." In a nutshell, this is what Stoicism is all about. It states that adaptability is a key trait that will lead to a happier life. However, when you have less adaptability, you start to feel unhappy very quickly when something does not go your way. Yet, no matter how bad things get, you do not have to give in—remember that. Minor and major things will happen to you, and you can deal with them in exactly the same way using the technique of emotional resilience. If you are still unsure of how to implement this behavior in your life, consider developing the following useful habits:

- **Don't Take Everything Personally** - This is difficult, especially when the situation directly involves you, what you stand for, or your actions. If you find yourself constantly being attacked by negativity, think to yourself that this is not your fault. You are not solely responsible for what happens to you or what someone does to you.

For example, if someone insults what you are wearing or is rude to you, it may be that they are experiencing their own negative feelings that have nothing to do with you. It's important to see the bigger picture of events and to understand that there may be other factors involved. Having this perspective allows you to not take events or experiences so personally.

- **Face Any Fears That Are Lingering** - If you are worried about having a negative experience in regard to something you want or need to do, stewing in your pessimistic attitude will not make you feel any better. The Stoics believe that every single experience can become a lesson learned. There is value in taking chances and even risks.

So, do what you need or want to do and then learn from your experience. Show yourself that not all of your fears will come true if you decide to branch outside of your comfort zone every once in a while.

- **Seek Out Spiritual Guidance From Within** - Spirituality and religion are not the same—you do not have to be a devout follower of any organized religion to be a spiritual person. What this means is that you can look inward and use your best judgment and intuition to guide you instead. Trust your gut instincts when you don't know what to do. Consulting them can bring you great peace of mind.

Most people do not realize that this is the reassurance they need.

Meditation can enhance your practice of spirituality. Being quiet and alone with your thoughts for a few moments each day can allow you to regroup. It will bring all your fears and worries up to the surface so you will have a better understanding of what you are feeling and what you need to do about them.

Being of Service

To be of service means to do good for other people. When you know how to treat yourself right and how to respect who you are as a person, you will be able to better interact with the people around you.

As an example, your partner is someone you know very well. You understand their boundaries, what they like, and what they dislike. A sense of their core beliefs should be clear to you. Being of service to your partner does not always mean doing extravagant things for them. You do not need to buy them a gift every day to prove your love for them. Instead, focus on what might improve their life in a subtle yet thoughtful way. Making the bed because they couldn't in the morning is a helpful and meaningful action you can take. This shows that you care about them, respect your living space, and want to be of service.

For a child, it is easy to equate being of service to buying material items. Children love receiving gifts on all occasions, but this is not the way to have a great relationship with them. To be of service to your child means being a present and active parent. Express to them how you are willing to listen to what they have to say, even if they feel like it is unimportant. Listening is a much-appreciated service you can give to anyone, but it especially helps children feel that they are important and cared about. You can also lead by example—model your behaviors after habits that you would like your child to pick up on. Since early childhood is a very developmental age, they are going to seek guidance from you at all times, even when they are not deliberately asking for it.

Friendship is another area of your life where you can be of service to other people. Since a friendship does not rely on attraction or romantic connection, communication and support are the languages you speak. Make it known that you care about your friends by always listening to them and asking how they are doing. Give them advice when they ask for it, using your empathy to fully understand the perspective they are coming from. Of course, when a friend needs a favor, try to be there for them to the best of your ability. If you know that your friend is going on a trip, offering them a ride to the airport is a simple and helpful act of service you can provide.

In a professional environment, you are more focused on your own actions, as you should be. You must prioritize your time when it comes to your livelihood. And while doing an act of service for your boss or peers can seem counterproductive when you have a workload of your own to focus on, there are still opportunities for service. If you experience a moment where you have some free time, you can ask a coworker if they need any help finishing up a project. You can also offer to take on additional work if you are available and your boss is looking to delegate tasks. Simple things like offering words of encouragement can also be considered acts of service. If you notice your coworker nailed a presentation, let them know. This is a kind gesture, and it will also build their confidence.

You can also be of service to complete strangers who you encounter. This is an ultimate act of selflessness, and it falls in line greatly with Stoic principles and beliefs. If you see another human who needs help and you have something to offer, reach out to them. By extending your offer, this is an act of service in itself. They might not require the help you think they need, so do not automatically assume your service will be changing a flat tire or paying for the money that someone is short at the grocery store. Sometimes emotional support is all someone needs.

What defines a great act of service is the intention behind it. Showing other people that you are giving and kind gives them an idea of who you are and what you believe in. You have no obligations to strangers, but choosing to act in their service will promote humble qualities in yourself. In turn, this can show you how to appreciate yourself even more than you already do. You have so many redeeming qualities, both to offer yourself and to the people around you.

Stoicism in the Workplace or at School

Applying Stoicism to any aspect of your life is going to give you peace of mind—this is one of its ultimate goals. When you are content with what you are doing and what is going on around you, this makes you a more productive and motivated person. Of course, in workplace and school settings, productivity and motivation are mandatory. You must be able to put your personal problems aside and focus on the information you are being given and the tasks you must complete. This ability will deem you either a successful employee/student or someone who is struggling. Understandably, many struggle in both of these areas of life. If this sounds like something you have experienced, the principles of Stoicism are here to help.

To explore more about how to be Stoic in the workplace and in educational settings, consider these quotes by famous Stoic philosophers. They will help you relate Stoic principles to your daily life, and we will then discuss how to make them work for you.

"Frame your thoughts like this—you are an old person, you won't let yourself be enslaved by this any longer, no longer pulled like a puppet by every impulse, and you'll stop complaining about your present fortune or dreading the future." —Marcus Aurelius

Interpretation: Stated in *Meditations*, Aurelius explains how you must use your wisdom as a guide through life. In both work and school, you must take a certain degree of instruction from someone who holds a higher role. This can pose a problem if you are someone who struggles with authority. Instead of rebelling against that authority, however, you can learn how to agree to disagree on certain subjects. Take a look at the bigger picture—you need your job to pay your bills and you need your education to get a better job.

Since these are beneficial tasks to complete, you need to have a little bit of give and take with each situation. You cannot let your emotions control or lead you down the wrong path. Manage your emotions with resiliency and learn how to put away your personal problems while you are in a professional setting. By staying focused on what you are doing at the present moment, you are more likely to succeed.

"If it is not right, do not do it. If it is not right, do not say it."
—Marcus Aurelius

Interpretation: You must rely on your moral compass, even when you are at work or school. When placed in a group situation, it is easy to get swept away by peer pressure. You might find yourself on board with something that you are morally against. It is okay to challenge other's beliefs in these situations. If something truly feels wrong, be the one to speak up about it—this is the Stoic lifestyle. You never know whose mind you might open up by simply stating your opinion.

"Some things are up to us. Some things are not up to us." — Epictetus

Interpretation: If this seems like a matter-of-fact statement, that is because it is. You do not get to control everything while in a professional environment. Not only do you have supervisors, but you must also take into consideration the feelings and opinions of your coworkers or peers. Let it go if you are not the one in charge. You can still practice your own great Stoic habits while doing work that is independent of or guided by other people.

"Many things have fallen only to rise to more exalted heights." —Seneca

Interpretation: You might lose a promotion to a peer or you might fail a test that you studied hard for—these are challenges in life that Stoicism prepares you to face. When you fail or fall, this does not mean that a downward spiral is your certain fate. There are many instances when people have failed miserably, only to come out on top because of persistence and willpower. Don't lose sight of who you are through your professional struggles—your self-worth is not connected to your job title or your test scores.

"At the end of the day, none of the criticism or the accolades changes anything real in my life." —Nita Strauss

Interpretation: Do not take the stress of work or school home with you. If nothing can be done about the situation now, there is no use holding onto that negativity. It can be very hard when you are worried about a missed deadline or an upcoming project, but you need to learn to let these things go. They do not change who you are as a person, and they do not indicate that you are going through a life-altering experience. The same can be said for the praise you receive and the success you reach—when you focus too much on these, you lose your ability to be humble. When your ego takes over, it can have a negative effect on you.

Parenting

Parent

Though the ancient Stoics could not have predicted the parenting techniques of the future, their methodology still works well for raising a child today. Not to be mistaken with uptight parenting, Stoic parenting focuses on instilling as much wisdom into the child as possible. In Stoic thought, parents are teachers who are responsible for teaching a child how to behave, think, and learn. While children go to school, they still learn a lot from their parents at home. The Stoics believe in teaching their children about self-care, values, and responsibility. They do not believe in raising children who grow up to disrespect, so discipline becomes a necessary life lesson.

When it comes to praising children, the Stoic philosophy warns that too much praise can affect a child negatively. They also saw that it had little utility. Some Stoics, such as Marcus Aurelius, believed that you should never or rarely praise your children. This might sound absurd in today's modern world, but there are reasons behind this way of thinking. Aurelius simply warns that you must carefully and deliberately praise your child. Do not praise them for doing simple things that they should be doing anyway, such as doing their chores or cleaning their room—praise is like a reward, and rewards should only be given when astounding actions are performed.

In Stoicism, praising your children should happen after they try, fail, and then learn. Urge your child to try something, even if a positive outcome is not assured. The praise should follow when they keep trying, though it isn't going well for them. This shows resilience and determination, two wonderful traits that the Stoics sought. Instead of saying, "You are so smart!" in this instance, a Stoic would say, "You worked so hard!" This will send a very clear message to your child why they are getting praised. It will encourage them to try again, building their self-esteem.

Kids are going to frustrate you. They will go against your wishes and challenge your patience. Sometimes, you might feel like giving up entirely and letting them run around freely without any rules because that seems easier than disciplining them. Instead of losing your temper when your child is acting unruly, you need to turn your focus inward. The goal should be to make it a learning experience for both of you. Consider that the failure might be on you, not on your child. You taught them certain behaviors, or they saw you perform certain actions; they might simply be learning by the example you are setting. Consider this before you punish them.

Maintaining a healthy, positive household is up to you. As the leader of the household and as the parent, you must reassure your child that there is always a reason to feel gratitude. Remind them of how lucky you all are to be together and have what you have. While they might have a lot of wants and desires, their survival needs are being met with a roof over their heads and food in the fridge. Remind your children that things can always be worse, that some do not even have homes to return to or schools to learn in. A change in perspective will show your children how to be thankful.

When your child learns what gratitude is, you can make it a part of your family's normal routine. Sitting together at the dinner table, go around talking about what each of you is thankful for. Turning this into a family activity both strengthens your bonds and helps to keep you all humble. It is a small reminder that the principles of Stoicism are not only meant for adults—children are very quick to pick up on these principles, too.

Like any parenting strategy, Stoicism agrees that children must be punished when they do something wrong. Instead of automatically getting angry, stop and ask the child why they misbehaved. This should be your first step in determining what punishment is suitable based on what happened. Often, a child acts out from a place of hurt or heightened emotion. Through understanding their perspective, you will be able to give them advice or wisdom so that the same problem does not happen again.

Your kids will throw tantrums, giving into their feelings of greed. They will ask you for toys or games, and you will have to tell them "no." It is important to stay strong as a parent; remember that you are in charge. Receiving guilt trips from your children is something that shouldn't happen. You must reinforce your role as a parent by being a great leader. Teach your children that they can't always get what they want but they have what they need. The more you give in, the more you will be spoiling your children. You need to give into their wants sparingly because then they will appreciate what they have a lot more.

Continuing Your Journey

Path

To continue your journey toward Stoicism, you do not have to do anything in particular other than living a virtuous lifestyle. You will know what it feels like the more you implement Stoic principles into your life. First, however, consider what you would do in every situation that you typically rely on autopilot for. These automatic responses are what we can change to fully embrace the Stoic lifestyle.

Some real-life examples you can use are below:

Situation: Your partner wants to do something with you over the weekend, but you want to stay home and clean up around the house. This causes tension to form between the two of you because your partner says that they feel you no longer want to spend time with them. You argue back that your partner does not value your home or help you take care of it. You find yourself at odds about the situation.

Stoic Solution: Instead of starting an argument with your partner on the matter, each of you must turn inward and remind yourself of what your core beliefs are. Do your core beliefs still align? Is there a way you can clean up around the house before you go out for a few hours? There are always solutions to be found if you are willing to look for them. Fighting without a purpose is not going to teach you anything valuable.

Situation: Your child sees a commercial on television for the latest bicycle. They already have a new bicycle from their birthday this year, but the commercial tempts them. They ask you for the new bicycle, and you tell them "no." This results in a temper tantrum with some verbal onslaught about how you are not a fair parent. If you really loved them, you would allow them to get the bicycle.

Stoic Solution: This situation would likely make you very angry, but remember to stay calm. Teach your child the value of what they have by reminding them that some kids do not get to ever ride a bicycle during their childhood. Teach them to appreciate the one they have now, cherishing the fact that it was a birthday gift picked out with love. You do not need to go directly for the punishment because your child is acting out; they are behaving this way because they are experiencing greed. More anger does not make greed dissolve, but humility will.

Situation: You were planning on spending the day at the park with your family, but you woke up to a surprise thunderstorm. Disappointed, you begin to complain about the weather and how it has ruined your plans to have a great picnic and some time in the sun. You feel aggravated with nature, and this puts you in a bad mood for the rest of the day because you don't know how else to spend your time.

Stoic Solution: Appreciate that nature is offering the trees and flowers water on this day. While this did change your original plans of having a picnic, you can spend time indoors with your family. Set up the picnic blanket in the living room and eat the same food you were planning on eating outdoors. Play board games together while enjoying one another's company. There are still ways to turn an unexpected change into a great day to cherish.

Situation: Your neighbor comes home one day with a new car. It is similar to your sedan, but it has a leather interior and a shiny paint job. Greed fills your mind as you watch them pull it into their garage. You feel mad that you cannot afford a new car and irritated that you have to drive a car that is several years old. The greed that fills you causes you to treat your neighbor differently. When they wave in your direction, you scowl.

Stoic Solution: Feel grateful that you have a car. While your neighbor might have a newer model, that does not mean your car is inferior. Your possessions do not define you as a person. Practice your humble attitude by admiring their new car and complimenting it. The fact that they have something you want does not mean you cannot have the same thing in the future—you must make priorities and work toward your goals.

CHAPTER 4
CRITICISMS TO STOICISMS AND COUNTERARGUMENTS AGAINST THOSE CRITIQUES

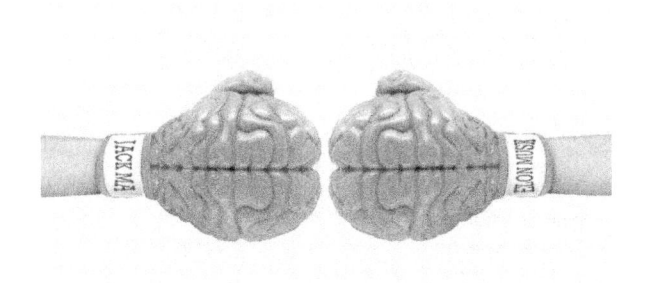

Debate

While any Stoic would gladly be willing to describe to you in detail all of the wonderful benefits of following a Stoic lifestyle, there are many who disagree. These critiques go as far as to say that Stoicism is not only ineffective but a terrible way to live your life because it will not lead you to true happiness. In this chapter, these critiques will be explored and explained. You will also be able to read the counter information to the critiques in order to get a full picture of both sides of the argument. After all, information is knowledge, and you can never have too much.

The "False Promise" Argument

The Ayn Rand Institute believes that Stoicism endorses determinism, which gives us false expectations. The practice of Stoicism states that some things are up to us and some things are not, but the Ayn Rand institute argues this viewpoint is so strict that it appears nothing is truly up to us. We must settle for what we see and what we appear to know, being unable to change the courses of our own lives because Stoicism tells us to simply go with the flow. Their problem with Stoicism is that there can be no consistency because nothing is truly up to the human race.

Stoicism *does* state that our judgments and actions after an event are up to us, but these reactions will not change the so-called fate of what is already occurring. If someone is married and unhappy, they might react by fighting with their spouse. One would think that this fighting might be a contributing factor to their future divorce, but Stoicism argues that this fate was not up to the individuals themselves.

Without any casual power, we humans essentially cannot affect events that happen to us or around us. It takes away the feeling of collective energy and purpose that humans seem to share on a daily basis. What Stoicism teaches instead is how to accept the inevitable, as there is no other choice in the matter that can prevent a certain situation from occurring. The Ayn Institute believes that philosophy must preach that we have some genuine control over our actions if it is truly meant to be a "guide" to life.

Counterargument

Stoicism only appears to have a strict deterministic view to those who do not fully understand it. On the outside, it appears that humans must take on a sit-back-and-let-it-happen type of attitude regarding events that happen in life, but this is untrue. While the statement that "some things are up to us and some things are not" is indeed a Stoic principle, this does not mean humans are helpless. While some challenges are thought to be of divine intention, Stoics believe other situations can change depending on how we react to them.

The point of letting go of control is to free yourself of the stress and burdens you might be holding on to. And a lot of stress comes from worrying too much about things that you cannot change. The Stoic lifestyle helps people let go of the notion that putting negative energy into a person or situation will change it. Stoicism wants us to repurpose that energy into something positive and, if we can achieve peace of mind by simply letting go, then this is the more favorable option.

If the Stoics believe in one thing it is that humans are *not* helpless beings. They believe we have power beyond what we know. Their casual approach to its use, however, is what confuses people. Stoics do not simply sit back and watch life unfold. They are purposeful and wise, only exerting energy when they know their words, actions, behaviors, or judgments will make a difference in the situation. They believe this is how we become strong enough to handle the challenges that come to us. If we were reactionary in every instance, this would eventually wear us down.

The Value of Emotions Argument

Feelings

Eric Scott, who is a philosophy blogger, poses an argument that the Stoics' combined beliefs concerning virtue and emotions suggest that we should essentially avoid emotions that are tied to the attachment to external items, ideas, and instances. He concludes this from an ancient Stoic doctrine known as *Apatheia*. He states that this is a complex topic, however, and the doctrine is ambiguous when it comes to distinguishing "good" emotions from "bad" emotions. It appears unclear if there are any good attachments or if all attachments are considered unhealthy.

Based on his theory, one can assume that a lack of attachment indicates a lack of involvement—this suggests a rather passive lifestyle while following Stoic principles. No matter how it is viewed, there is an underlying suggestion that we must tame our emotions. What comes naturally to us is not inherently natural and can be altered. Some principles even ask us to eliminate certain emotions. The purpose of this is to direct all of the energy we have toward the events we "can control." This leaves Scott feeling perplexed, because it suggests we should be void of attachment to our loved ones, our safety, and our wealth—common things in life we become easily attached to.

When it comes to compassion, this becomes an even greater issue. Scott believes that it is our moral duty to be automatically compassionate, empathic, and understanding of perspectives different from our own. He quotes ancient academic Stoic philosopher, Crantor, as an example of this belief:

"I cannot by any means agree with those who extol some kind of impassivity (apatheia). Such a thing is neither possible nor beneficial. I do not wish to be ill, but if I am, and if some part of my body is to be cut open or even amputated, let me feel it. This absence of pain comes at a high price; it means being numb in body, and in mind scarcely human."

Scott posits that Cantor's suggestion is valid in the sense that removing the capacity to feel comes at a cost that is too high, and it is not healthy to give up the emotional parts of ourselves because this is what makes us inherently kind individuals. The world does not revolve around us, so why would we neglect to think about other people?

Counterargument

The idea that Stoicism teaches us to completely disregard our deepest emotions is one of the biggest misconceptions about this philosophy. Stoics are seen as resilient and strong, but this does not mean they don't love their families and enjoy spending time with their friends. Their main priority is not to channel their deepest emotions into these interactions, however. It is to channel them into what is best for the greater good—a state of virtue that will lead to the Good Life.

Stoicism is much more than simply redirecting emotions inward. The purpose of being careful with the use of emotional energy is to build up your resilience and to be able to handle life's challenges.

Compassion is something that Stoics believe in, but it is not the central guiding force behind the philosophy. In most arguments against Stoicism, people are quick to express that compassion is not a priority; this is untrue in some ways— while it might not be at the top of the list of priorities, it exists because the Stoics believe in being humble. You can only learn how to be humble by practicing the art of compassion, and Stoicism does promote acts of service. If you can do something that will lead to the greater good, you are encouraged to do so.

The Stoics *do* wish to free their mind from any worries, doubt, or negativity, but this does not come with a high price to pay. It is done in a gradual manner that teaches you how to manage your emotions by turning them into positive self-serving behaviors. This is not to be confused with the action of selfishness, though. As mentioned, the Stoics enjoy performing acts of service for those in need. They are kind people, and they value compassion and empathy in ways that might seem a little far removed according to the average thinker.

The Uncertainty Argument

Scottish philosopher David Hume points out that Stoicism functions on the foundation that everything that happens in the universe is rational and orderly. He has a problem with this theory because there is no way it can be proven. He gives the example that if a car hits his daughter, killing her, Stoicism would encourage him to have faith in the divine plan—the challenge that was just presented to him by the gods because they know he can handle it. While this might be possible, Hume disagrees that this has anything to do with a rational universe because you must have faith that the universe has a plan in the first place. Believing there is a plan is only your own mental perception of the way the universe works.

Hume, however, agrees with some points of Stoicism. He admits that it is within the nature of the universe to create and destroy, and that Stoicism offers some consolations for that natural aspect of the universe. Everyone is going to die because this is how mortality works. Some of us will live long and healthy lives, while others will be taken far too soon. He believes these thoughts are rational and, in this way, they align with Stoic principles. However, he departs from

Stoicism with the belief that we live in a deterministic world—whatever happens, we must go along with it because it is not an event we can control.

There is no karmic influence in Stoicism, like that in Buddhism, which Hume views more favorably. If his daughter were to get hit by a car, the Stoics would not suggest that she did something in life that would cause her to be met with bad karma. Instead, they would merely state that this is an instance we cannot control, and it happened. There is little explanation of *how* or *why*, and this is what bothers a lot of people about Stoicism. Often, humans crave more information than they are given, but this need for more can be viewed as greed according to Stoic principles.

Another argument Hume makes is that he feels uncomfortable with the way that the Stoics view passions. In Stoicism, essentially, all passions are seen as disorder. Even the passion of wanting to be compassionate toward other people can be viewed in a negative light, and that is something Hume argues against wholeheartedly. He does not understand how there can be anything wrong with being a kind and compassionate human being.

Since Stoicism focuses so much on outward events that happen to us that we must accept, Hume worries that this promotes a general sense of apathy and quietism. In this modern world, remaining passive on certain societal issues can present a problem because it can mistakenly suggest that you side with the oppressor.

Counterargument

The main point of Stoicism is to train yourself to accept what you cannot control, so you have no need to feel panicked or worried by events that happen to you or around you. Still, you *can* control select elements in your life. But to some, this can seem like a very passive way to view the world.

It is not that the Stoics do not care about the events they cannot control; they just choose to accept that they cannot do anything rational or real to change a situation. In doing this, they are able to let go of their worries and fears—this is what causes them to appear so strong and unphased by hardship.

Stoicism warns that life *can* be uncertain at times, but this is not always how they view the world. Only certain instances that are difficult or challenging are uncertain, but this is why they work so hard to reach a point of acceptance. They do not want to be hindered by these events in the future. When you hold onto difficult moments or emotions for too long, they start to influence the way you think, feel, and act. For example, if you lose a loved one and never accept or process that this happened, you are going to notice changes in your behavior. Everyone needs their own individual time to grieve, and it should never be rushed, but Stoicism would suggest handling these emotions as soon as possible.

The Stoics are very aware of vices because they can get in the way of reaching virtue. When you are caught up in a vice that stems from passion, you are going to take several steps back from being on the path toward the Good Life. The Stoics are not preaching that having passions is inherently wrong or bad, but they do teach you that an abundance can result in some unfavorable outcomes in your life if you are not careful.

By not stemming all passions, you run the risk of

encountering negative or harmful emotions. Lust is not merely the feeling you get when you admire someone, as it can transform into rage if the one you admire starts dating another person. These passions, then, will not lead you to become a kind or compassionate person.

Overall, Stoics accept the uncertainty of the world, but they do the internal work of learning how to be okay within the chaos and irrationality of what is outside of them.

Stoicism in the 21st Century

To make more sense of these arguments and how they might directly apply to your life today, it helps to hear personal stories about how Stoicism fits into people's 21st century lives. With any ancient practice, changes and adaptations have been made to Stoicism to make it more relevant to modern times. While Stoicism is not a religion, it does include a lot of principles that are, admittedly, outdated. Even if you are not following the exact steps of ancient Stoicism, adapting its principles without changing the meanings will serve you well.

Many people today, mostly working professionals, incorporate Stoic habits into their lives to make them more productive and effective. As discipline is key to success, they have found that Stoicism has helped them develop this skill. To find success, practicing Stoics today have used the below Greek concepts as guiding principles:

Apatheia: the freedom from your emotions to be without suffering

Ataraxis: a state of tranquility that makes your emotions impenetrable

Autarkeis: the ability to maintain your inner freedom

Control of feelings, tranquility, and inner freedom help Stoic professionals navigate their work life successfully. In the workplace and in your personal life, conflicts can arise fairly easily. However, Stoicism encourages you to think before you act. This can prevent you from encountering problems with other people or internal conflict with yourself. It can be hard to not act in a reactionary fashion, but this is exactly what Stoicism teaches. This principle applies to the 21st century just as much as it did back in ancient Greek times.

Askesis refers to a form of self-discipline that focuses on mastering who you are as a person. This is another very helpful element of modern-day Stoicism that can be applied to nearly every aspect of your life. It is thought that being the "master" of your own life can lead to some incredible results. Since nothing has power over you to hinder you or hold you back, you should essentially be making the best choices possible. This is a challenge in today's society, especially with societal pressures affecting your decisions. With Stoicism, you will have the strength to resist the things you know are not good for you.

Below, you can read about some modern-day Stoics who have used the principles of the philosophy to find success:

Tim Ferriss

An entrepreneur and author, Tim Ferriss considers himself to be a modern-day Stoic. He focuses on the topic of Stoicism for entrepreneurs in order to help them learn about successful business habits that will lead to profitable outcomes. After writing several books on the topic, he has become widely recognized as a leading modern Stoic. *Tao of Seneca*, his most recent book, gives insight into how to deal with high-stress environments, such as the workplace. He advocates for using Stoicism as a tool in your daily life. After learning about what you can control and what you cannot, Ferriss believes this will allow you to remove stress from your life, just as the ancient Stoics taught. He also strongly advocates for the idea of self-mastery and becoming your own leader. Through this practice, you will become less impacted by the criticism that you are bound to receive.

Ryan Holiday

Much like Tim Ferriss, Ryan Holiday is an entrepreneur and author. His book, *The Obstacle is The Way,* is based on the Stoic belief that one must frame all obstacles as opportunities. He also put together a meditation booklet that outlines several Stoic meditations, which is called *The Daily Stoic*. Among his Silicon Valley counterparts, Holiday is well-known for bringing the philosophy of Stoicism back into the 21st century. He also incorporates the modern concept of podcasting to spread the messages and beliefs of Stoicism. His feature on *The Stoic Entrepreneur* addressed how Stoicism is often viewed negatively. It is misconceived as being a negative or depressing philosophy that has a lot of limitations. Holiday explained that Stoicism is really just very practical and pragmatic. Because there is no dwelling on negative emotions, it is easier to understand and accept when things do not go according to plan.

Pete Carroll

An unlikely modern-day Stoic advocate, Pete Carroll is an American football coach who is well-known for his time working with the Seattle Seahawks. He explains that his coaching style is directly linked to Stoic principles that he also uses in his personal life, and he firmly believes that they have made him a better coach. Through realizing that he has a lot of inner grit himself, he learned how to teach his players how to find the same inner grit. The Seahawks were defeated in Super Bowl XLIX by the New England Patriots, but through the wisdom Carroll learned by reading Holiday's *The Obstacle is the Way*, he led the team forward instead of being battered by an onslaught of negativity. From his coaching style to the way the team had played in the Super Bowl, there was naturally a lot of criticism received. Through applying Stoic principles to this situation, Carroll helped the team keep moving without becoming hindered by what they were hearing in the press.

CHAPTER 5

PREPARING PRACTICES

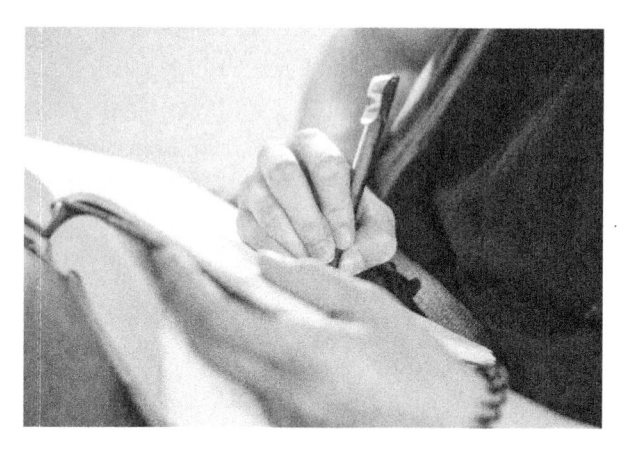

Lesson

In Stoicism, practice is essential. Learning about the principles is not going to be enough to transform your life. You do not need to practice each one with repetition or time-consuming action, however. By incorporating the principles you want to maintain in your life, you will slowly take them on as habits that feel natural. To do this, it does require you to tap into your sense of self-discipline. Ask yourself why you are doing this and how you wish to accomplish it. If you do not have a clear goal in mind, this is not going to give you much motivation to put in the effort of adopting a more Stoic way of being.

Whether you want to feel more at peace in your daily life or understand how to better understand your emotions and social interactions, you already know how Stoic principles can influence you. Like anything that you want to become great at, Stoicism is no different—it takes determination to succeed. Learning how to be Stoic is not something that revolves around the idea of passing or failing. The entire process becomes a lesson you will learn from every step of the way.

To begin, write down a few goals that you have that are inspired by Stoicism. When you write them down, they become more tangible. Put the list in a place where you will see it daily.

As you read through some of these practices, remember that you do not need a definitive deadline for each one. Setting an estimated deadline can be helpful in terms of motivation, but do not set yourself up for automatic failure. For example, it wouldn't be realistic for you to change your entire life in one week. Remember, a new habit takes about 21 days to form. Give yourself time to fully understand and comprehend the necessary changes you wish to make. Along the way, your feelings might also change. You will encounter both setbacks and victories, but it all becomes a part of your overall experience.

Remind Yourself of Impermanence

Nothing in life is guaranteed. Consider this example: You need to get milk from the grocery store, so you get into your car and start driving. While your intention is fully focused on arriving at the store and buying milk, it is still not a guarantee that you will come back home with it. Why is this so? Maybe you will arrive at the store and it is all out of milk. Maybe you will get a flat tire on the way, causing you to take a detour to your local auto body shop. You never know what might happen to you, and this is exactly how you can think about the term "impermanence."

This theory is not meant to scare you or make you paranoid that something bad will surely happen—it is merely a rational approach to thinking about the events that happen in your life. If you get too carried away with the "what-ifs," don't forget to balance this out by also imagining the best possible outcome. Using the above example, maybe you will arrive at the store and they will have an abundance of milk available. As you get in line to make your purchase, maybe the person in front of you will feel gracious and offer to pay for your milk out of the kindness of their heart. This would be a wonderful outcome, and it is just as possible as the other two negative examples of what might happen.

When you think about the way that nothing is a guarantee, not even your own life, this is going to shift the way you think. In life, there are many inconveniences that appear that make you feel frustrated, annoyed, or devastated. To change the way you react to events, you must practice more gratitude. It will make you feel more appreciative of each day you get. Try taking a moment before you get out of bed to reflect on what you are thankful for. Reminding yourself of what you already have will show you that you are still lucky in many ways and will remind you to consider the greatness that is in store for you, just waiting around the corner to be discovered.

When something amazing happens, Stoicism does not state that it was merely luck or chance. Deliberate action plays a big role in this philosophy. While you cannot always control each given situation, you do have the power to make the most of what you can. Essentially, Stoicism teaches you how to look on the bright side of life, always seeking the silver lining in the impermanence. Many people are under the misconception that Stoicism teaches you that you should not care too deeply to avoid feeling disappointment. Through its principles, you are actually going to care very deeply. You are going to care so much that you create a purpose behind everything you do.

When you think about the things that you have missed out on in the past, do not dwell in these feelings of disappointment or despair. The past is called the past for a reason—it already happened. What you need to focus on is what you can do right now, in this impermanent moment, that will create a more positive result. The same concept can be used when you are grieving the loss of a loved one. You miss them so much, but this is one of the unfortunate situations you cannot control. They are gone because life is impermanent—it is a reality we will all eventually face. Appreciate the great times you had with them and understand that each person is put into your life for a reason.

The next time you find yourself caught up in feelings of

annoyance or disappointment, give yourself a gentle reminder that this experience is impermanent and is happening to you because it is a lesson to be learned. You are lucky to be the recipient of such an experience, even if it challenges you. Gentle reminders that you are still fortunate will get you through these temporary setbacks. Because the world is ever-changing, even right now, you should find solace in knowing that anything can change at any given moment.

Whether you consider yourself a religious or spiritual person or you simply hold other beliefs, there is no denying physics and biology. As the Earth is revolving on its axis, this is a constant that you can rely on each day you wake. The whole reason you are here right now is that the Earth was given another chance to revolve. When you are feeling hopeless, even with no will to live, you can always think about something bigger than you—there is nothing bigger than the planets or galaxies. Remind yourself that your problems are not the biggest parts of this picture that is your life. While they impact you greatly and shape you in many ways, you can get through this temporary situation. Know that all is impermanent.

Reminding yourself of impermanence will also allow you to appreciate those in your life more often. Seeing the people you love every day is not a guarantee, as you already know. Appreciate the value they add to your life and the lessons they teach you. Understand your role in their lives and how you fit into their bigger picture. Considering how interconnected we all are is an amazing experience. A single action that you make can enhance someone's entire day, maybe even their entire life. This is a powerful thought to ruminate on.

Contemplate Your Own Death

Grave

This concept seems morbid to many, but it can become a great preparation practice as you delve into the world of Stoicism. Building off the previous concept of impermanence, it is a fact that your life is also not a guarantee. We all die; it is part of nature's way. As the Stoics are very connected to nature and follow its patterns closely, they see birth and death as a natural cycle. As such, death is not something that you need to spend a lot of time fearing. Life and death are both profound moments that happen to every single person on the planet. It is a shared collective experience that can make you feel more connected to the people around you.

To contemplate your own death in your daily life, you need to do this properly. The topic can become easily depressing if you are only focusing on the fact that, one day, you will die. This is setting aside a lot of other factors involved, such as the wonderful life that you have the potential to live between birth and death. For this practice, the following three strategies are all great for contemplating life and death in a healthy way.

Death is All Around You

Each day, take a few moments to look around and observe your surroundings. Notice everything that once had life but is now dead. You can view the plants, flowers, and trees on your way to work. Some of them might be thriving, but there will be others that have reached the end of their time—this is death. This is a way to think about death without depressing yourself or scaring yourself. View it for what it is: a natural part of all life. You might recall a particular tree that you climbed as a child that is no longer on this Earth, but its memory remains.

If you are indoors, you can look at material items in the same way. The cotton clothing in your closet once came from a plant that was alive. The cotton was harvested, and now, you have a shirt to put on your back. The wooden coffee table that you rest your mug on came from the wood that used to be a tree. Leather objects that serve purposes in your home came from the sacrifice of an animal that was once living.

The idea is not to punish yourself or make yourself feel bad for the daily death you encounter, but to bring awareness of its impact and importance. You will notice so many "dead" things each day, which will normalize the idea that you will meet the same fate one day. It is normal, natural, and expected. It is a constant in life that will not let you down, though you cannot predict the exact moment when everything will change.

What Will Outlast You?

In the same way that you used observation to complete the previous exercise, look around you at the things you know will outlast you. This can be an interesting concept to ponder because it is unlikely you have spent much time doing so in the past. You might notice buildings and houses that will continue to stand on their foundations after the day you die. Maybe certain restaurants and shops will remain open to customers. The general theory is that all life does not stop for one death. Even objects of minimal significance will likely outlast you. For example, a pen that sits on your desk might still exist after you die.

This can be taken as tough love, or it can be used to grow your appreciation for what is around you.

There are children that will outlive you, perhaps children of your own. The generation after you will likely continue to live on, shaping the world that they live in. While you will not be around to see it, this does not mean you should feel bitter or upset—this is a selfish approach. Feel joy in your heart that generations to come will get the chance to learn and grow just as you have. While they might do things differently, their impact will be felt by the generation that comes after them—just as your impact will be felt.

When thinking of death in this way, you will learn to appreciate that every object, event, and person plays a unique role in the world. And while you may be gone, there are still parts of you that live on.

Contemplate Death in Times of Illness

When you fall ill, you can take this time to contemplate your death. This idea sounds especially morbid, but it does not have to be. Your health is not a guarantee. Think about the last time you caught a cold. It likely came out of nowhere, hindering you and your ability to function on a basic level.

When feeling ill again, consider that your good health is not an automatic given. This can be a humbling thought. It can lead you to the realization that each day you have in good health is a day to be thankful for.

As you lie in bed feeling ill, this is a great time to contemplate the temporary element of life itself because you are already feeling a fraction of what it means to slip away from the Earth. With a weakened state of being, the person you are is only a shadow of the way you normally function. Listen to all the sounds you hear as you are in bed. Reflect on the idea that these are the things that will continue on as you slip away. Feel appreciative of the moments that you got to spend outdoors and exploring new places. Understand that experiencing nostalgia can make you happy.

Even if you feel lethargic, like you might truly die, don't forget to tap into your Stoic strength. Tell yourself that you will get through this illness and pay attention to the notion of your survival instincts. You will not simply lie in bed and waste away, not if you can help it. You do have a choice in the matter of how you will take care of yourself if you are ill. If you are not capable of caring for yourself, accept the care that others offer.

Negative Visualization

When introduced to the term "negative visualization," most would probably assume that this means focusing on all the bad stuff that has happened or could happen. It is a much more practical process, however. Negative visualization helps you to foresee the bad stuff that might be coming your way. In a sense, it is the activation of your intuition. Have you ever had a bad feeling about a situation, only to find that something bad does happen? This was your gut instinct warning you of something negative. In Stoicism, listening to these feelings and being in touch with these emotions is very important.

If you can use negative visualization as a tool, it will help you make better decisions in your life. If something feels wrong, then there is a reason for it. Even if you cannot inherently identify what is wrong about it, your gut instinct will not lie to you. Something might be clashing with your moral values or core beliefs; maybe you are being put into a situation you do not agree with. Try to trust your gut instinct as much as possible. If you are unfamiliar with the process, it might be difficult to let your apprehensions go, but this is the start of Stoicism.

The idea of negative visualization can feel very counterproductive if you are unsure of your end goal. Take this example into consideration: Imagine you arrive at work, ready to get started on a big group project that will result in a large win for your company, but you feel unsure about it. Your boss walks into the conference room with the announcement that the project will ultimately be a gigantic failure. You look around in confusion and disappointment because you have not even started yet. This brings up feelings of how hard you were planning on working and how much you wanted to see the whole thing through—you wanted success.

It seems like a strange approach, and to many, it is. This type of visualization works, though. In the above example, the sudden negativity that was encountered brought up all of the positive feelings that you were planning on putting into the project, maybe they were even feelings you weren't consciously aware of. It reminds you of what you stand for and how your actions could have impacted the overall result.

You can use this theory to help you appreciate every other aspect of your life. Seneca used to rehearse his future travel plans in his head or in writing, imagining all that could go wrong. Maybe a big storm would hit, causing delays, or causing him to be unable to complete the journey. Perhaps, he could fall ill. Or maybe, the captain of his ship might be attacked by pirates. Anything negative that could happen, Seneca would rehearse it.

In doing so, he was giving himself plenty of opportunities to think critically. Imagining each one of these scenarios, Seneca was able to figure out what he *would* do if faced with one of the adversities he came up with. While it is impossible to prepare for all of them and, of course, the results are not guaranteed, it is still a productive use of time because it requires a lot of rational thinking.

When you work on the idea of a potential disruption in your plans, you take on Seneca's approach of being able to handle either victory or failure. When you are prepared for each of these polarities, you will automatically be able to handle anything else that happens in between. While a pleasant surprise in your plans is much more favorable, this practice teaches you that you do not have to shun the negative surprises. Do not avoid them or rebel against them. Remind yourself of the Stoic principle of welcoming anything that comes your way. In an instance when nothing can be done to alleviate the negativity, you will be okay because you have prepared for this. It is a situation you have no control over, but you can remain calm and levelheaded about it because of the negative visualization efforts that you have made. The idea is to prepare yourself for anything and everything.

To put it in very simple terms: This will suck, but it will ultimately be okay. Most people learn the hard way that the world is controlled by several external factors. They try so hard to change certain situations or events that cannot be changed, only to be disappointed. In Stoicism, acceptance is the key. Your negative visualization will help you accept anything that happens.

If you are constantly surprised when something negative happens, because you are not yet desensitized to it, then you are going to feel miserable more often than not. You will also have a much harder time accepting what is happening and how you must deal with it. By opening your mind to the idea of Stoicism, you will learn that desensitization can be a very good thing.

The way you use your mind changes a lot when you shift into Stoicism. It takes on a more proactive role in everything you do, from the way you get ready in the morning to the way you handle rejection. The Stoics believe in the power of the mind almost more than anything else. They recognize how much power lies within being prepared and thinking clearly.

Consider Everything as Borrowed from Nature

In Stoic belief, you do not actually own anything. Everything you have within your possession is simply borrowed from nature. Whenever possible, it is thought that you must also return it to nature when you are done with it. One of the simplest examples of this idea is recycling. When you are done using your plastic bottles, you recycle them so they can be reused, and new bottles can be created from them. The same idea goes for composting: When you return uneaten or unused food scraps to the Earth, the soil will receive its nutrients and thrive. The Stoics always believe in giving back this way because they aim to live in the most natural way possible.

However, you can still enjoy what you are currently borrowing. Appreciate it when you have it because it can be taken away at any given moment—this overlaps with the theory of impermanence. You will not always be considered in these decisions, nor will your feelings. What gets taken from you might die, or it might become broken and unable to be used for its intended purpose. Maybe someone will steal it out of their own greed. You never know what might happen to the things and people you love, but you can always circle back to the idea that everything is borrowed from nature.

When something you enjoy is taken from you, this can feel like a personal attack. It might make you want to act out in rage or revenge, but you must refrain from giving into these passions. Instead, center yourself by remembering that it did not belong to you in the first place. It can be incredibly difficult to let go, but you can give yourself consolation by believing maybe nature needs it more right now. It will also remind you that you cannot give into your greed; be thankful for what you had and when you had it.

The Stoics believe that it is pure ignorance to think that you will be in possession of anything forever—nothing is forever. Opening your mind to a new way of thinking can help you cope with loss, a very necessary skill for anyone to master. Create awareness around the idea that nature can ask for something back at any moment, and we must oblige because we are only the borrowers. We need to respect nature and follow it through its course. There is no halting a system that has been in place for centuries. Disrupting this system is only going to make the process of acceptance harder for you.

When you truly cannot imagine something being taken away from you, it is easy to believe that it *cannot* happen to you. This makes it especially hard to deal with loss when it inevitably occurs. The Stoic principles teach that you must train to accept and welcome misfortune—this is why negative visualization is seen as a helpful tool. This is meant to soften the blow and make you aware that you are not immune to the bad things that happen to so many people in the world.

Not acknowledging that everything is borrowed leads to ignorance. And ignorance is only bliss for so long. Eventually, you will have to face losing a person, a thing, or yourself. Maybe a loss is not impacting you at the moment, but it is happening to someone you know—eventually, you will be able to relate to the misfortune. Anything that happens to your fellow man can also happen to you, and this includes negativity and loss. Just because nothing has happened to you yet does not mean it won't. It also doesn't guarantee it will—that is the point. You need to be aware of the fact that it *can*.

While exploring the idea that everything is borrowed from nature, you might be thinking about something like your house or your car and how they fit into this theory. These structures and vehicles are made from materials that are borrowed from the Earth. Whether it be steel or concrete, the basic components do come from nature. If your car breaks down in the middle of the road and is unsalvageable, this is a moment when you can reflect on nature deciding to take it back. Appreciate it for all the places it has taken you and then make a plan of action for your future transportation.

Imagine your house burns down—this seems a lot harder to accept, and it is. Still, the concept that nature loaned you the home will help you get through this hardship. Seek solace in the idea that nature knows exactly what it is doing. It has known for over millions of years, so put your trust in it. Feel the emotions that you need to feel, then make a plan to better your life and obtain the basic survival items you need. Getting stuck in a rut is entirely possible when a huge, negative life event happens. This is why it is a good thing to have an explanation for why even the worst things happen to you.

Remind yourself to respect nature and its decisions, always.

The Stoic Morning Routine

Below is a Stoic morning routine you can use in your own life:

- **Bed** - Before you can do anything, you must get out of bed. This is a simple, first step to take in order to get your morning started. The way you get out of bed matters. If you trudge along and shuffle into the bathroom to prepare for your day, this isn't going to give you a positive or uplifted feeling. If you snooze your alarm clock, lying in bed for an additional 10 minutes will also not do anything to enhance the day ahead—this simply delays the possibility for action.

  As a Stoic, you must commit to your decisions. Once your alarm goes off, get out of bed, and then make your bed. This will teach you some self-discipline.

- **Showering** - Even if you do not choose to take a shower every single morning, on the days you do, you can use this time to prepare your mind for what is to come.

  Make sure your mood reflects your upcoming actions. If you have a lot of work to do, you need to stay focused on these tasks that await you. Get into the mindset that you plan on getting a lot done. Tell yourself that you are resilient and that you can handle anything that comes your way.

- **Dressing** - The Stoics do not believe in extravagance that is expressed through style choices. The clothing you wear is merely a protection against the elements.

It should be practical, comfortable, and appropriate for the occasion.

This is not to say you cannot embellish your outfit with your own creative style choices, but you do not need to spend too much time on this practice.

- **Eating Breakfast** - Nourish your body with basic foods that will allow you to function at your best. When you fill-up on sugary or carb-heavy meals first thing in the morning, this is going to slow you down both physically and mentally.

Remember, Stoicism encourages you to take care of yourself in both ways, and nutrition is a very important element to beginning your day.

- **News** - It is not within the idea of a Stoic lifestyle to get on social media and read the news first thing in the morning. This is going to stimulate your mind too much, causing you to use brain power that you might want to delegate on other tasks.

There will be a better time and place for catching up with news and events when you get a break from the things you prioritize.

- **Mental Warm-Up** - Getting your mind ready for action is highly recommended. You can think of your day as a sports game, and your mind is the tool that will be used in the game.

To succeed in anything strenuous, this requires a warm-up of some sort. There might be a lot of thoughts circling your head about your tasks ahead, but let them pass on. Instead, focus on your skills. Tell yourself how strong and capable you are. Understand that you are going to enter your day with the best mindset possible.

CHAPTER 6
SITUATIONAL PRACTICES AND HOW TO HANDLE YOURSELF WHEN CHALLENGED BY OTHER PEOPLE

Conflict

Facing challenges that involve other people is an incredibly common occurrence in life. Through Stoicism, you can learn how to handle these events in the best way possible. When you are emotionally-driven, you might find yourself more prone to acting in a reactionary manner. For example, if your friend cancels plans on you at the last minute, your first instinct might be to feel upset with them. Maybe you even express to them that they are selfish for canceling, which then leads to an argument between you that causes you more anger and sadness.

Practicing Stoicism, however, allows you to handle situations that involve others in a way that will not cause as much negative emotion. When you can learn to process your emotions before projecting them onto other people, both of you will be a lot better off.

Thinking like a true Stoic, remind yourself that nobody owes you anything. Your friendship is not based on favors or tasks that you must do for one another. While this is only taking the above example into consideration, becoming humble in your approach to handling challenging situations that involve other people will help you stay calm. It will lead you to rational thought rather than emotionally-driven outbursts that you might later regret. As you read on, try to tap into your ability to be as humble as possible—teach yourself that not everything is worth conflict or a confrontation.

Find Your Own Faults

To further practice the art of being humble, you need to remember that you have faults of your own. You are not a perfect being; nobody is. Consider that your faults are also contributing to the challenging situations you are dealing with that involve other people. The idea behind this is not to berate yourself or to ruin your self-esteem, but it serves as a reminder that you need to take accountability for your actions.

Reading the below example, see if you can identify with this situation:

You have a small dinner party at your home, and you invite friends over from different groups. Your childhood friends are there, some of your coworkers are there, and your spouse invites some of their friends, too. At the table, an argument arises between a long-time friend and a coworker. They have different political opinions, so they get into a heated discussion that makes everyone else at the table feel uncomfortable. You do your best to try to mediate the situation, but it just keeps escalating. Eventually, you take the side of your childhood friend out of loyalty. Your coworker becomes angry at this decision, acting negatively for the rest of the dinner party. The next day at work, they are giving you the silent treatment.

Confrontational situations can be incredibly uncomfortable, especially when you are put in the middle and are only trying to keep the peace. If you take sides, you then have one person who feels supported and another who feels betrayed.

What is the next step you can take in this situation?

First, remember that the problem did not begin with you. In this case, the altercation took place between two other individuals. What you need to look at is the moment you got involved and the actions you took. What started as an attempt to fix the situation turned into an involvement that led you to choose sides. Only taking your actions into consideration, you need to see if there are any decisions that you must take accountability for that might have contributed to the negativity.

For example, maybe you should not have handled the situation in front of the rest of the people at the dinner party. This made everyone uncomfortable, and you could have asked the other two people to step into another room to try and resolve the matter.

Maybe you also should not have given into the pressure to pick a side. You could have remained a mediator, as intended, while fairly hearing both sides of the argument before coming to your conclusion.

Now, you must consider if you owe an apology to your coworker. Of course, this is a personal decision but think about the way you took action and see if that apology might be warranted.

Your flaws might not be as prominent as your strengths, but Stoicism will remind you that you still have them, and it is okay to have them. When you practice Stoicism, you are on a constant journey to learn more about yourself and how to carry yourself in a way you can be proud of. Maybe the way you handled something was a mistake, but you know what the Stoics think about mistakes: Learn your lesson, and use the information that you learned to help you react better next time. Give a heartfelt apology, if necessary.

Many feel that this is a common way to handle a situation like the one described above, but Stoicism asks you to take things one step further. Do your best to identify your faults. Not only do you need to remedy the situation, but identifying your faults will help you to turn them into strengths. You gave into peer pressure, so that is a fault—you were easily swayed. You got confrontational because you saw other people becoming confrontational—this escalated the situation. It isn't easy to look at what is "wrong" with your behavior, but it will help you grow and evolve.

Remember, the goal is not to make yourself feel bad about the flaws you currently have. This process is meant to help you identify how you can make yourself a better person. It will teach you more about your values and beliefs. This also keeps you humble, reminding you that you aren't always going to be right—you won't always be wrong, either.

In some cases, it isn't even about being right or wrong. The lesson learned might be as simple as seeing that there are other perspectives to consider besides your own. This is a very important life skill to have, and it will become useful to you in nearly every situation you encounter with other people, regardless of if it is positive or negative.

Forgive and Love Those Who Stumble

You need to have compassion in your heart at all times. Forgiveness is a hard concept for most because being hurt by someone is difficult to process. Whether your partner does something wrong or a friend betrays you, these are moments of weakness that are being displayed by the other person. Even a stranger can do you wrong, such as cutting in line in front of you at the store.

All these situations become challenging in very different

ways, but they all incorporate the idea that you must learn how to handle them, regardless. If you constantly get upset about each instance where something bad happens to you, then you are not going to live a very happy life. The Stoics would even argue that you would never be able to live a virtuous life.

To learn how to forgive someone, consider these steps to help you open up to the idea of forgiveness and why it is important:

- **Know What It Is and Why It Matters** - Can you define forgiveness? Maybe not as easily as you thought. You might be able to let go of situations that do not matter to you or impact you much, but true forgiveness is the intentional act of letting go of and understanding a situation that deeply hurt you.

    In any capacity, forgiveness is important because it alleviates the burden of holding onto the event and thinking about it. When you live with that much negativity in your heart, it becomes very distracting and can become debilitating.

- **Change Your Inner Monologue** - If you say you want to forgive someone, yet you are still thinking negatively about them or the situation, then true forgiveness is not going to be possible. Your mindset always needs to line up with your actions if you want them to be genuine.

    This does not mean you must automatically accept what has happened to you, but you should work at processing it. Figure out why it makes you feel bad and how you can move forward from it.

- **Address Your Pain** - Before you can forgive anyone, even if it was for something seemingly trivial, you must deal with the pain you are feeling. If there is still active pain in your heart, then you must address it.

Thinking about it can be scary because it might feel like you are going through the situation all over again, but this is how you will fully heal and be able to reach a place of forgiveness. Do whatever needs to be done personally to handle the pain you are feeling. Reach out to someone or consult a professional if you feel that you need more help with your mental health.

- **Rely on Empathy** - When you have sorted through your personal feelings, take on a stance of empathy. This means that you can think about the situation again, but instead of automatically focusing on the bitterness that you feel because of what happened, you can look at it through an empathetic lens.

Some people are naturally more empathetic than others, but empathy can be learned. It takes an intentional focus to become a more empathetic person. Use this trait to guide you as you think about the situation. Consider where the other person was coming from.

- **Find Meaning in Your Suffering** - You were not suffering simply to suffer—there is always a bigger reason behind it. Find the lesson that you learned from the hurt you experienced. You might have gained more resilience, or you might have discovered who you can trust in your life right now.

No matter what the lesson is, make sure you understand that each situation that challenges you comes with one. Pay attention to it, and make sure you can take away something from the experience other than pain or suffering. If you only see the experience as a deliberate attack on your happiness, you will continue to feel bitter about it.

- **Forgive Yourself** - You are hard on yourself because you are your own worst critic. Self-forgiveness is just as important as forgiving the person who hurt you. This gives you a complete picture of how you are going to move forward in your life.

When you are able to forgive yourself, this is a true testament to the fact that you honor who you are, which is a belief in Stoicism that should be followed at all times. Not only must you honor your values, but you also need to honor the person you are. Be proud of yourself and your decisions, even if they are not always the right ones. This will lead you toward a path of forgiveness.

Nobody Errs on Purpose

You might feel insanely frustrated with someone who wrongs you—this is natural. In your mind, they chose an action that impacted you negatively. In your anger and upset, you may even believe they did this on purpose. Some people are quick to point fingers of blame and to think everything is purposeful sabotage. You need to rely on your humble mind to remind you that nobody makes a mistake on purpose. If you were wronged and you conclude that a true mistake was made, then you must also understand that this person did not deliberately set out to harm you.

Of course, there are instances when people act with malicious intent. You have experienced deliberate, hurtful actions that have shaped the person you are today. It is difficult to predict whether or not someone in your life will end up hurting you, but if they do, you can determine if the intention behind the action was deliberate or accidental—this truth will guide your decision making about what to do next. When you find that someone made a mistake that resulted in you being hurt, this is your chance to remind yourself that you could have made the same mistake.

You do not have to accept their wrongdoing simply because they made a mistake, but bearing in mind that the other person did not take an intentional action toward harming you will help you remain open-minded to the situation. Mistakes happen very easily, and how the other person handles the situation is also very important.

When you see how careless people can be, even those you consider yourself to be very close to, this can change the way you view people. Naturally, you might see someone you thought to be very kind as selfish once they upset you. Were they truly acting in a selfish manner, though? This is what you need to identify to find your own truth. A selfish person acts with only their own well-being in mind. They will not hesitate to bring others down if it brings their happiness up. Is this the way you were treated?

Being able to answer this question will further help you figure out if the wrongdoing was purposeful or if it was a mistake. When someone expresses to you that they made a mistake and they try to apologize to you, do your best to hear them out.

It can be very hard to give someone this chance, especially when they hurt you, but consider that you would want the same treatment in return if the situation were reversed. Do your best to hear what they have to say without jumping in with an emotional reaction. Yet, even without an apology, you can find solace in the fact that it was a mistake. At the very least, this will provide you with some peace of mind that you deserve.

Even though mistakes are made by other people, there are lessons for you to learn. Maybe you will realize who you should be spending time with and who you should distance yourself from. Or maybe, you will find that this person simply had a moment of bad judgment and that you can fully forgive them. No two situations are exactly alike, so do your best not to compare your past to your present. This puts unfair pressure on an already challenging situation.

Try to use a fresh lens each time you evaluate a situation. Of course, your past does play a role in the way you see things, but this is your present. In Stoicism, living in the present is very important. Because Stoic principles always talk about bettering yourself and reaching the highest virtuous form of living, you need to remind yourself to continue living in the present. This can prove to be challenging, but it is just one more aspect of your life that you will work through and that will make you even stronger.

Find Pity Rather than Blame

The idea of pitying someone is probably familiar to you, in a sense. When you feel pity for someone, this implies that you are compassionate, in some way, to what they are going through. If someone hurts you and you realize they have caused this harm because of an internal struggle they are going through, this doesn't make it okay—it does, however, give you the option to pity them rather than blame them. Blame is not a very productive emotion. For one, it is very negative. When you blame someone for something they did wrong, you are not suggesting that there is a fix or a resolve that can be found afterward. To blame someone is to basically tell them that they were in the wrong and that you feel negatively about them.

As you try to sort through your conflicts with other people, work on finding pity instead of blame. Before you say anything accusatory, stop yourself for a moment to think about where this anger is coming from. Of course, there was something bad that was done to you. In some ways, placing blame on this person can feel like you are getting back at them. This is not a healthy way to manage negativity, though. Getting revenge on someone might feel great in the moment, but it is not a long-term solution that you should rely on.

This topic goes along with the idea of instant gratification—it feels great, but it does not last. If you want to become more Stoic, you must think of practical and rational solutions. Getting revenge on someone who hurt you will not lead you to any form of lasting happiness. Instead, it will simply keep hatred in your heart, which will make its way into other aspects of your life. Overall, placing blame should always be avoided. There are always other options when it comes to dealing with emotionally difficult situations.

Stepping away from a situation for a moment to reflect on it will help you come to a more rational conclusion about it. If you stay in a heated argument for long enough, you are bound to say something you will regret—anyone is. It is a mature sign for two people to be able to have a conflict and then take separate time to think about what just happened before forming a reactionary final response. While it isn't always possible to take a moment to think about what to do next, seize these opportunities when you see them. Use them to reflect both on the situation and your own feelings.

Once you have had some time to think, your anger will slowly subside. While you still might feel very upset deep down inside, that first stage of anger or rage should be tamed. Now, you will be able to react in a way that is much better than what it would have been at the beginning of the situation.

Remember to rely on facts when you are sorting through problems with others, and only use the "I" statements. If they have made you feel a certain way, you can begin explaining this by saying "I feel" instead of "you did this, so now I feel…" Blame always exacerbates conflict, so it is best to do what you can to manage any further damage.

Speak calmly and evenly when you do discuss what happened. If you do not end up receiving an apology or with an outcome that you hoped for, this is something for you to handle on your own. You cannot change someone's mind, even if you know their thinking is flawed. What you can do is find your own sense of inner peace. Do what you can to make sure that you are okay, even when the other person is being difficult to deal with. Some conflicts will remain open-ended solely because the other person is too stubborn to deal with it. This will be difficult, but you must know when to stop trying and when to focus on handling your own emotions.

From what you now know about Stoicism, you know how important it is to only focus on what you can control. Understand that what happens to you might not be fair or right, but you do not need to take on a victim mentality. You will use this moment to become a stronger, more resilient person. You will learn your lesson from the experience, and you will learn how to simply pity the one who hurt you. Even if you completely disagree with their actions, you can pity the fact that they cannot find a way to move forward from the situation. Pity allows you to live your most virtuous life.

How to Deal with Insults

An insult is not always going to come in the form of hurtful words that are spoken about you directly. An insult can come in the form of questioning your intelligence or knowledge. It can also be a subtle act, like when someone makes a certain facial expression after you say something meaningful or when they ignore you altogether.

There will be many people in your life who attempt to insult you or belittle you in an effort to manage their own insecurity. People who are deeply insecure tend to put others down because this makes them feel less terrible about themselves. Unfortunately, you might find yourself as the subject of someone's insults one day. This can be difficult to manage because your first instinct is likely to fight back in the same manner. Stoicism warns that we should not be this reactionary, though. There are much better ways for you to handle insults that will not damage you emotionally or psychologically.

There are six basic responses to any insult, some good and some unfavorable. Below, we will consider each one and determine why some of them are better than others:

- **Anger** - This is a weak response. It shows the other person that you immediately internalized the insult, implying that you do not think very highly of yourself. It showcases the truth behind the insult, if any.

  It also upsets you very much, causing you to take actions that you might not have taken before you became debilitated by the insult. When the insulter knows they have gotten to you, they will be tempted to insult you again because they know it already worked once.

- **Acceptance** - This can seem like a weak response, but it might be one of the strongest responses you can muster in return. When you hear an insult, you will immediately consider if it is true and where it comes from. If you find that the insult is somewhat true, this can become a valuable lesson.

  Sometimes, people insult you with no truth to back up the statement. In this case, you can still learn from it and move on with your life; do not give the insulter the satisfaction of response—this is still acceptance.

- **Returning the Insult** - No matter how quick-witted you are, returning an insult is only going to do one thing: provide the insulter with an invitation for conflict. When you return an insult, this might also put you at risk of worse treatment because the insulter is usually very fragile to begin with. When they see you acting out in an aggressive manner like them, they are going to take this as a challenge.

   What started as a backhanded remark can turn into an altercation very quickly. You need to become the bigger person instead of stooping down to their level.

- **Humor** - When people feel uncomfortable, some rely on humor to get them through the situation. The reaction of humor can be hit or miss when it comes to insults, but it is still useful to try.

   If it is successfully timed, it takes away the power from the insulter and diffuses tension. Some people find success in adding to the original insult. While you might not believe what the insulter said is true, it is still going to be surprising to them when you jump in on the action and make fun of yourself.

- **Ignoring the Insult** - When you simply ignore the insult and move on, this can become a very effective strategy. As long as you are truly able to get over it and not let it impact you negatively, ignoring the insult is a perfectly fine way to respond.

   It does not give the insulter the satisfaction of knowing how you feel about what they said, and it does not humor the situation at all. As you move forward from the insult, the insulter might be confused, even wondering if you heard them.

- **Rebuking the Insult** - If you hear a statement about yourself that is simply untrue, you might have no choice but to jump in and defend yourself. If you decide to rebuke an insult, try to remain focused on the facts—state your case, and try not to let your emotions take over.

While you might feel very upset by what just happened, when you state facts, it makes a much more powerful argument. The insulter is going to feel challenged in a great way when you make a point that they simply cannot argue. It takes a lot of calmness and grounded energy to be able to do this successfully.

CHAPTER 7
STOICISM IN PAIN MANAGEMENT

Pain

Pain is inevitable—it is a part of human life. Sometimes, it comes in the form of a lesson to be learned or from a direct response to your actions. You can always learn from the pain you feel, but first, you must learn how to successfully manage it.

There are different types of pain that stem from different events you experience. You might accidentally physically hurt yourself and or maybe someone else will physically hurt you on purpose. Often, you will experience emotional pain. This type of pain usually hurts more than physical pain because it lingers. No matter what causes your pain, your end goal should be the same: to stop the suffering.

In Stoicism, there should be no suffering. Anything that is challenging happens to you for a reason, as you know. You need to accept what is happening, learn from it, and move forward in your virtuous life. If still holding onto pain and suffering, you will not be able to accomplish this. Many people wonder why they cannot live up to their own expectations or complete their goals, and they eventually learn that their past is holding them back. The pain and suffering that was once felt is still lingering in the background.

Through learning how to use Stoic principles to manage your pain, you will find the methods that work best for you. They will not always be the same for every person, as human beings are very diverse. The better you are at managing your pain, the easier it will become to understand the pain that others feel. In turn, this makes you a more empathetic person. Overall, pain management is a very important skill that most people never learn. Even if you feel that you are lacking in this trait, it is never too late to teach yourself what is necessary for your survival.

Physical Pain

Marcus Aurelius was an expert at pain management. He used

Stoicism to cope with his illness and chronic pain. Before he became a Roman emperor, it was already known that Aurelius struggled with pain and pain management. In a letter he penned to his Latin rhetoric tutor, he apologized for his shaky handwriting, blaming it on his lack of strength and pain in his chest. Not in the best physical condition, Aurelius developed four methods for managing his pain that were based on Stoicism.

Separate Your Value Judgments From the Sensations

Earl of Shaftesbury was an early modern Stoic who came up with the "sovereign precept." What this represented was that it is not the things that upset us but the judgments we have about them. Take a broken leg, for example: Imagine you have just broken your leg. Sure, you are going to experience physical pain, but you will likely be able to survive this experience. After the physical pain subsides, you might feel judgments toward yourself about your worth. Now that your leg is broken, you can no longer drive your children to school. Though they can take the bus or ride in the carpool, this still upsets you because you feel that you have failed in some way.

It was not your choice to break your leg, therefore, you should not extend your pain and suffering by putting yourself down because of it. When you separate the judgments that you have about your self-worth from the actual physical pain you are experiencing, this is going to help you get through it a lot better. When practicing this method, you will find that the physical pain no longer feels as bad because it is not being further exacerbated by the weight of emotional upset.

Marcus Aurelius followed this concept closely in his quest for pain management. He would explain physical pain as nothing more than a "rough sensation" in the body. To describe something as a sensation is to imply that the feeling is fleeting. Because it is a fundamental Stoic principle that any sensations felt are to be seen as neither good nor bad, this should get you through the rough times when you are experiencing any type of pain. After all, it is a fleeting sensation.

Consider the Consequences of Good vs. Bad Coping

When it comes to coping, you can either choose mechanisms that will improve your well-being or hamper it. When you consider the consequences of both actions, you are building motivation for change. Since you are doing a comparative analysis of your options, you are likely going to make the better choice because you will see how many positive benefits choosing a good coping mechanism will bring you.

The Stoics created a similar technique for weighing options. To practice their technique, they reminded themselves of the paradox that comes with feeling anger or sorrow toward a situation. When something physically hurts you, feeling angry about it is only going to make you feel even smaller and less in control of the situation. You might even start to feel helpless about it, given time. On the other hand, if you do not let yourself get caught up in such feelings of doom and anxiety to begin with, you can focus on your main goal: getting through the pain and getting better. Weighing these options, it's obvious which one is best.

In Stoicism, it is thought that pain actually does no real harm because it cannot change our moral character unless we allow it to do so. While it might cause us physical distress, we still hold onto the same values on the inside; this is what keeps a Stoic so strong through any physically painful situation. It is a promise of truth to be kept and held onto. Real pain that lasts stems from any decision we make to hold onto or to dwell on physical pain.

How Awful is the Pain?

Think about the pain you are feeling. Is it going to end the world? When something hurts you, it upsets you—this tends to increase the intensity of the situation. In doing so, the event will appear more harmful or threatening to you. We have all hit our shins on a coffee table before. This is very painful, and it can cause a great deal of momentary upset in our lives. This is not the worst pain we have ever felt, but in that small moment of time, it can feel like the pain is going to end us entirely. As we come to our senses, we realize how small this situation is in the grand scheme of things. Of course, we will not allow a coffee table to derail our lives.

The Stoics do not catastrophize everything, but they do explore other areas of pain as a comparison. Through this thought process, they ask themselves if they are capable of enduring something worse. Considering the above example, it is almost unquestionable that you would agree you can endure worse pain than hitting your shins on the coffee table. Maybe you have already. If you are having trouble thinking about your own experiences, consider the experiences of others. There are others out there who have definitely endured worse pain.

This strategy is not meant to invalidate your feelings but to put them into perspective. When you realize that the physical pain is not as awful as your mind is making it out to be, you will sooner conclude that you will survive it. While this can all seem very dramatic, this is how the human brain works. You need to be very deliberate with your thought process to get the results you are after.

What Ability Do You Have to Cope?

Lazarus' theory of stress is modeled after a seesaw. According to his theory, psychological distress occurs when you have an imbalance between two factors: your perceived ability to cope and the perceived severity of the threat.

Imagine you are injured in a cycling accident. You were wearing a helmet but falling off your bike meant you endured many scrapes and bruises. During your healing process, you find out that your injuries are not very serious, and your true prognosis appears positive. You can easily upset yourself by overthinking what you have been through, however.

If you feel that you cannot cope with the pain that comes from your bruises or you feel that the fall from your bike is going to hinder you from ever cycling again, this is going to put you in a state of psychological distress. Once you are there, your physical pain is going to feel amplified. You might start to believe that your body will never be the same again, further upsetting you and putting you into an even deeper and darker place in your life.

You need to pay attention to the way you think. Instead of focusing on your weaknesses or what you are currently incapable of, you can use Stoicism to rely on your strengths. Remind yourself of exactly what you are capable of and bring up past examples as real-life reminders of you being able to get through difficult situations. Your physical pain should not ever bring you to the point of an emotional collapse. You must remain as strong as you can.

Emotional Suffering

Crying

When you are in emotional distress, you are sensitive to everything around you. Even minor challenges, such as encountering traffic on your way home from work, can send you into an emotional tailspin. When you feel distressed and vulnerable, the bad things in your life are going to appear more amplified than ever before. This is very upsetting because it can lead you to believe that you cannot get through this moment in time. You might feel frozen in place, stuck in a feeling of despair. While this can sound very dramatic, it is so easy to fall into a deep depression because of it. Your mental health should always be taken seriously, no matter how trivial you perceive the situation at first.

Stoicism teaches you how to be strong and grounded. You are supposed to handle your emotions with ease, reminding yourself that what you are feeling isn't always necessarily what is true. When you are suffering from great mental distress, even mental illness, you are not going to be able to think as clearly. Your mind will be cluttered with thoughts about how bad off you are and how weak you are. Going down this path is like jumping into a rabbit hole of negative feelings. It becomes so easy to spiral out of control, and it makes you unable to ask anyone for help.

You are going to encounter emotional suffering in your lifetime, as you already have on numerous occasions. The Stoics posit that it is not what happens to you that defines you but how you react to it in return. Through finding Stoic coping mechanisms that make you stronger, each emotional moment you experience will no longer hinder or debilitate you.

Here are five methods for coping with the emotional stress you experience in your life:

Mindfulness

Great emotional stress is an indication that you need a way to empty your mind before you reach a breaking point. The act of mindfulness will help you with that task. Whenever you start to feel "heavy," take a moment to listen to your mind and body to discover where your true upset is coming from. This heavy feeling can be prominent in your heart or chest, but it can also manifest in your stomach. Notice how all pain and suffering seem to connect, somehow as well. What starts as a physical ailment or sensation will eventually turn into an emotional one.

Instead of trying to run away from your feelings, be brave, and stay. When you use mindfulness instead of escapism, you will learn a lot more from the experience. Open yourself up to your deepest feelings, but have a purpose while doing so. Make your purpose the quest to discover clarity and a solution. Do not let these negative emotions take over you completely.

Acknowledge what you are feeling and why. This might take some time, but you must be patient with yourself. Once you have this figured out, you can set the emotion free. Imagine you are making room for more positivity in your life, and visualize the emotion floating away from you. Through this process, you will find that you are less burdened by your troubles.

Distraction

You were likely taught that distractions are always negative, but they can be helpful at times. If you can feel yourself settling into a pattern of negativity, use a distraction to redirect your energy. What matters most here is what you choose to distract yourself with. As long as the activity is productive and beneficial to you in a positive way, it will do the job. Replacing an uncomfortable feeling with a destructive distraction is not going to do you any good; be mindful of this fact.

An example of some good distractions might be to take on a

creative project or to teach yourself something new. Spending time with the most positive people in your life can also have a wonderful impact on your emotions. A distraction isn't meant to be a solution to your problems, but it can help you clear your head until you are able to think of one. Remind yourself that it is okay to take breaks.

Once you complete your fun or relaxing activity, you can go back to the situation you were previously dealing with. Notice how you feel a renewed sense of energy to put toward it. Using distractions to rejuvenate yourself will ensure that you are doing everything you can to process your emotions in a healthy way.

Blocked Time

Distractions do not work for everyone, but there are more strategies you can try. Blocking off time is something that works well for people who feel the need to be on a schedule. When you allow a distraction into your life, this can feel like you are giving up too much control. Blocking off time in your schedule will allow you to feel less guilty when you need to step away from an emotional challenge.

Make sure you give yourself an hour each day to do something kind for yourself. Whether you want to practice an act of self-care or try one of the positive distractions listed above, know that this scheduled time is for you to use as you see fit. This is your chance to unwind and let go of the things that are bothering you, even if it is only for one hour. Any space from the issue will help you.

If you feel yourself traveling back to the emotional challenge, remind yourself that you aren't going to be able to solve it without any fuel. Taking the time for yourself is your way of fueling and reenergizing yourself. Feeling run-down will not do you any good if your aim is to solve a difficult situation.

Meditation

Meditation is a classic activity that promises great results. Many use meditation to clear their minds or to stay balanced on a daily basis. No matter how you choose to meditate, it is worth a try because it aligns your mind, body, and soul—this itself aligns directly with the principles of Stoicism. When everything is balanced, you will feel better able to live your life to the best of your ability.

There are no rules when it comes to meditation. As long as you set some quiet time aside for yourself, you can practice it in whatever way you see fit. A lot of people choose to meditate right before they go to sleep at night or right after they wake up in the morning. These are two times when you will likely be able to focus well.

You can find guided meditations online, and there are numerous smartphone apps that are designed specifically for meditation. You can also guide yourself. Begin by breathing with your eyes closed, only paying attention to your breath. Once you find a steady rhythm, begin to focus on an intention. Depending on what you are focusing on, certain thoughts are going to rise to the surface—this is normal. Imagine that you are letting them pass through, not holding onto or ignoring any in particular.

You can meditate for five minutes or one hour—you need to figure out what works best for you. Meditation is a highly personal experience and the more you do it, the better you will understand which practices are most beneficial to you.

Therapy

Although the ancient Stoics did not have the option of going to therapy in ancient Greek times, you have the option now. Stoicism has evolved in many ways, offering solutions for even the most modern problems you might face. Your mental health is so important, and ancient Stoicism also recognizes this. You need to make taking care of your mental health just as much a priority as you do taking care of your physical health. If something does not feel right mentally, you are going to feel off balance.

Going to therapy can provide you an outlet. When you have a way to vent all your feelings and frustrations, you will be less likely to hold them inside. Allow yourself to, at least, explore the idea of therapy by trying it for a few sessions before you decide whether it will work for you or not. Meeting a therapist can be overwhelming at first, but it is their job to make you feel comfortable.

The therapist you are assigned should do their best to make sure that you are comfortable with the plan they come up with. Their aim is to help you, not to make your life any harder than it already is. Keeping your mind open is going to help you get the most out of therapy.

How to End Suffering

To ultimately end your mental and physical suffering, you must be willing to let go of it. Nothing is going to change until you make it a point to tell yourself you are letting go. Even when something is entirely negative, letting go can be very difficult. Having constants in your life, even constants that don't serve you, almost act as a type of security blanket. There is a strange comfort in knowing and accepting your own suffering. Suffering can even become a part of your daily routine, your daily thoughts, and that's why it is so hard to let go of.

But you deserve better than suffering—tell yourself this often.

Stoicism teaches you that you deserve to live a happy and fulfilling life. You must tell yourself this until you start to truly believe it. Write down positive affirmations and be very clear with your daily intentions. These small steps toward positivity will allow you to finally let go of what is causing you all this suffering. Through the process, you will have to learn how to forgive those who must be forgiven, yourself included. You need to be certain you have handled all the emotions involved. Then, you will be able to finally let go and keep moving forward.

Just because you let it go does not mean it will go away forever. Healing isn't a linear process. You might feel like you are doing very well for days or weeks at a time, only to encounter a challenging period of time. Remind yourself of what you can control, and use all of your resources to turn it into the best experience possible for yourself. At the very least, it will become a lesson to learn.

Keep reminding yourself that there is a better life for you out there that does not revolve around suffering. There is a life that is based on your passions and goals. You can turn your entire life around, even if you didn't realize you weren't living as the best version of yourself until recently; it is never too late to make a change for the better. Be gentle during this process. You are going to need time to adjust to what changes might occur. Also, reward yourself for any progress you make during this time—you deserve it. One day, you will look back at the time you spent suffering, and you will feel so proud of yourself for no longer being in that situation.

CONCLUSION

Now that you have a full understanding of the history of Stoicism and all that it entails, you should feel more confident about taking on some of these principles and turning them into lifestyle habits. Stoicism is so much more than just putting on a stern face and not letting negativity bother you—it is the idea that you can process your emotions efficiently and live the way nature intended to bring out your full potential as a human being. No matter what you are doing, there is a Stoic principle or belief to guide you. With a full understanding of the philosophy, you can now decide what parts of your life you can change to better yourself and your circumstances.

Though it began in the ancient ages, Stoicism has evolved a lot to fit a modern lifestyle. This is why so many successful people, such as business owners and entrepreneurs, adopt a Stoic lifestyle—it truly works. Stoicism keeps you organized and motivated. Because it helps you to understand how to process your feelings and how to let go of control of what you cannot change, there is more time to focus on meeting your goals. In turn, this makes you feel happier on a daily basis.

Stoicism is not a religion, though it has been around for a very long time. The principles and beliefs are meant to be used as an outline for living well. While some of them might not fit into your current, modern lifestyle, you might feel inspired to change some habits to see the difference it can make. Remember that Stoicism is about living your most virtuous life. When you live this way, you are going to reach your full potential and be on your journey toward the Good Life. You can think of this as the ultimate happy life that you are aiming to live.

Stoicism is suitable for anybody at any stage of life, as it presents a simple approach for building healthy habits and behaviors. If you want to be more self-disciplined and motivated, then you will enjoy what Stoicism brings into your life. Because the world can be a very uncertain place, it brings you a lot of inner peace, knowing that you can reassure yourself mentally and, therefore, perform better in your tasks and responsibilities. Your relationships and connections to other people will also improve because you are not burdened by your emotions. This leaves more room to connect deeply to others.

Above all, remember to enjoy your life—every moment of it. Stoicism teaches you how every single day can be a great day with a lesson learned, even when you face uncertain challenges or difficult situations.

You have made it this far in your life, so why not keep going? Stoicism gives you the strength to preserve, even while staring directly in the face of adversity. You can do this, and you will be proud of yourself for it. Welcome to your own path to the Good Life.

Leave Your Feedback on Amazon

Please think about leaving some feedback via a review on Amazon. It may only take a moment, but it really does mean the world for independent authors like me.

Even if you did not enjoy this title, please let me know the reason(s) in your review so that I may improve this title and serve you better.

From the Author

My mission as an author is to share all the knowledge and lessons I have learned over the years - these transformed me from a struggling employee, working 2 jobs and dealing with depression, to being worth over 5 million dollars and controlling my destiny.

I hope that with this knowledge, you are able to start transforming your life too.

REFERENCES

7 Benefits of Adopting a Stoic Practice in 2020. (2020, January 13). https://dailystoic.com/benefits-stoicism/.

9 Stoic Practices That Will Help You Thrive In The Madness Of Modernity. (2018, March 1). https://dailystoic.com/stoicism-modernity/.

99designs. (2018, March 21). *Stoicism for entrepreneurs: Practical philosophy for the 21st century.* 99designs. https://99designs.com/blog/business/stoicism/.

A Stoic Response To Desire. Daily Stoic. (2020, January 7). Daily Stoic. https://dailystoic.com/stoic-desire/.

A Stoic Response to Grief. Daily Stoic. (2017, September 25). Daily Stoic https://dailystoic.com/stoic-response-grief/.

Allan, P. (2017, September 1). *Parenting Advice From the Stoics.* Offspring. https://offspring.lifehacker.com/parenting-advice-from-the-stoics-1798673788.

Bidlake, E. (2019, May 14). *Remember you will die: 3 practices for contemplating death.* Erin Bidlake https://erinbidlake.com/remember-you-will-die-3-practices-for-contemplating-death/?doing_wp_cron=1597862813.4170730113983154296875.

Burton, N. (2013, February 13). *How to Deal With Insults and Put-Downs.* Psychology Today.

https://www.psychologytoday.com/us/blog/hide-and-seek/201302/how-deal-insults-and-put-downs.

Case Study: How Stoic ice baths helped a student reduce anxiety and procrastination. The Ancient Wisdom Project. (2017, April 6). https://theancientwisdomproject.com/2016/07/case-study-stoic-ice-baths-helped-student-reduce-anxiety/.

Creighton University. (2020, April 3). *How Stoicism can offer peace of mind during pandemic and beyond.* News Wise. https://www.newswise.com/coronavirus/how-stoicism-can-offer-peace-of-mind-during-pandemic-and-beyond/?article_id=729353.

Doesn't Matter What They Think, Only What You Do. Daily Stoic. (2017, July 19). https://dailystoic.com/only-what-you-do/.

Egan, L. (2020, May 29). *Stoicism: How This Ancient Philosophy Can Empower You to Improve Your Health and Your Life.* All About Habits. https://allabouthabits.com/blog/2019/12/05/stoicism-how-this-ancient-philosophy-can-empower-you-to-improve-your-health-and-your-life/.

Enright, R. (2015, October 15). *Eight Keys to Forgiveness.* Greater Good. https://greatergood.berkeley.edu/article/item/eight_keys_to_forgiveness.

Evans, J. (2007, May 16). *The problem with Stoicism.* New Statesman. https://www.newstatesman.com/blogs/the-faith-column/2007/05/stoicism-stoical-possible.

Garlington, B. (2019, June 8). *Be a Stoic to Win in the Workplace.* Attorney at Work. https://www.attorneyatwork.com/stoic-workplace/.

Garrett, J. (2003, September). *The Passions according to the Classical Stoics.* People.wku.edu. http://people.wku.edu/jan.garrett/stoa/stoipass.htm.

Here is a Pleasure You Can Have Anytime. Daily Stoic. (2019, December 24). https://dailystoic.com/here-is-a-pleasure-you-can-have-anytime/.

Humphreys, J. (2019, October 31). *How to deal with life's setbacks? Think like a Stoic.* The Irish Times. https://www.irishtimes.com/culture/how-to-deal-with-life-s-setbacks-think-like-a-stoi c-1.4062541.

Jaffe, A. (2018, May 22). *6 Easy Ways to Cultivate Positive Thinking Today!* Psychology Today. https://www.psychologytoday.com/us/blog/all-about-addiction/201805/6-easy-ways-cultivate-positive-thinking-today.

Massimo. (2016, February 5). *Stoic personal values: on luxurious living.* How to Be a Stoic. https://howtobeastoic.wordpress.com/2015/06/01/stoic-personal-values-on-luxurious-living/.

Piglucci, M. *Stoicism | Internet Encyclopedia of Philosophy.* Internet Encyclopedia of Philosophy. https://iep.utm.edu/stoicism/.

Quy, L. (2018, November 27). *Five Tips From The Stoics On How To Develop Mental Toughness.* Vunela. https://www.vunela.com/five-tips-from-the-stoics-on-how-to-develop-mental-toughness/.

Robertson, D. (2013, February 20). *Introduction to Stoicism: The Three Disciplines.* Donald Robertson.

https://donaldrobertson.name/2013/02/20/introduction-to-stoicism-the-three-disciplines/.

Salzgeber, J. (2019, April 12). *What Is Stoicism? A Simple Definition & 10 Stoic Core Principles.* NJlifehacks. https://www.njlifehacks.com/what-is-stoicism-overview-definition-10-stoic-principles/

Salzgeber, J. (2018, January 16). *You Don't Own Anything – Everything Is Borrowed from Fortune.* NJlifehacks. https://www.njlifehacks.com/you-dont-own-anything-everything-is-borrowed-from-fortune/.

Scott, E. (2018, March 11). *The Best Argument Against (and for) Stoicism.* Euthyphroria. https://ericsiggyscott.wordpress.com/2018/03/11/the-best-argument-against-and-for-stoicism/.

Smith, A. (2020, July 25). *The False Promise of Stoicism.* New Ideal. https://newideal.aynrand.org/the-false-promise-of-stoicism/.

Stoicism and Pain Management: *4 Techniques Practiced By Marcus Aurelius.* Daily Stoic. (2019, April 29). https://dailystoic.com/stoicism-and-pain-management/.

The Stoic Art of Negative Visualization. Daily Stoic. (2017, December 7). https://dailystoic.com/premortem/.

Toren, A. (2015, November 18). *5 Epic Leaders Who Studied Stoicism -- and Why You Should Too.* Entrepreneur. https://www.entrepreneur.com/article/252625.

Your Stoic Daily Routine - Zero to Philosopher in One Day. What Is Stoicism? (2020, May 22). https://whatisstoicism.com/stoicism-resources/your-stoic-daily-routine/.

IMAGE SOURCES

Ancient (n.d.). Retrieved from
https://unsplash.com/photos/-zoe4nviem4

Calmness (n.d.). Retrieved from
https://unsplash.com/photos/RFcjHE7J5SE

Cemetery (n.d.). Retrieved from
https://unsplash.com/photos/YSnZqsF4DLQ

Concepts (n.d.). Retrieved from
https://unsplash.com/photos/srCeIHW5Gtk

Conflict (n.d.). Retrieved from
https://unsplash.com/photos/e1daGOrmkIk

Crying (n.d.). Retrieved from
https://unsplash.com/photos/lQ1hJaV0yLM

Debate (n.d.). Retrieved from
https://unsplash.com/photos/nWDT7XoytTU

Emotions (n.d.). Retrieved from
https://unsplash.com/photos/ygrOmmn1Oss

Feelings (n.d.). Retrieved from
https://unsplash.com/photos/hbHkE-GSMfo

Grave (n.d.). Retrieved from
https://unsplash.com/photos/krqJ35KEcls

History (n.d.). Retrieved from
https://unsplash.com/photos/EHfiW-cV0ls

Lesson (n.d.). Retrieved from
https://unsplash.com/photos/neUbjUnjXNk

Morning (n.d.). Retrieved from https://unsplash.com/photos/IuLgi9PWETU

Pain (n.d.). Retrieved from https://unsplash.com/photos/mSXMHkgRs8s

Parent (n.d.). Retrieved from https://unsplash.com/photos/FqqaJI9OxMI

Path (n.d.). Retrieved from https://unsplash.com/photos/HiE1bIIoRqQ

Prayer (n.d.). Retrieved from https://unsplash.com/photos/lPCu8HnGU2E

Raven (n.d.). Retrieved from https://unsplash.com/photos/a1LVsvM_zuE

Smart (n.d.). Retrieved from https://unsplash.com/photos/mO9vKbG5csg

Thinking (n.d.). Retrieved from https://unsplash.com/photos/-wjk_SSqCE4

Printed in Great Britain
by Amazon